# THEN SINGS MY SOUL

# THEN
# SINGS
# MY SOUL

## 52 Hymns That Inspire Joyous Prayer

### PRAYER JOURNAL

## Robert J. Morgan

W Publishing Group

An Imprint of Thomas Nelson

Published in Nashville, Tennessee, by W Publishing, an imprint of Thomas Nelson.

Unless otherwise noted, Scripture quotations are taken from the New King James Version®. © 1982 by Thomas Nelson. Used by permission. All rights reserved.

Scripture quotations marked NIV are taken from the Holy Bible, New International Version®, NIV®. Copyright © 1973, 1978, 1984, 2011 by Biblica, Inc.® Used by permission of Zondervan. All rights reserved worldwide. www.zondervan.com. The "NIV" and "New International Version" are trademarks registered in the United States Patent and Trademark Office by Biblica, Inc.®

Scripture quotations marked KJV are from the King James Version. Public domain.

Scripture quotations marked TLB are from The Living Bible. Copyright © 1971. Used by permission of Tyndale House Publishers, Inc., Carol Stream, Illinois 60188. All rights reserved.

ISBN 978-0-7852-3655-9 (softcover)
ISBN 978-0-7852-3656-6 (eBook)

*Printed in the United States of America*

22 23 24 25 26  LSC  12 11 10 9 8 7 6 5 4 3

*To Tyler*

# CONTENTS

# INTRODUCTION

When my wife, Katrina, was weak and dying, I put my arms beneath her and lifted her from her wheelchair into her bed. She was a bit confused, but I heard her mumbling something that touched me to the depths of my heart: "My gracious Master and my God, assist me to proclaim, to spread through all the earth abroad the honors of Thy name."

Then she repeated the last line: ". . . to spread through all the earth abroad the honors of Thy name." It was a long-loved stanza of Charles Wesley's great anthem "O for a Thousand Tongues to Sing."

Katrina was whispering those words, almost subconsciously, as a prayer addressed to God, asking His help in proclaiming the glories of His name as long as she lived. She leaned on that hymn in death because she'd known it all her life. It was part of her lifelong internal collection of the great hymns—what I call her perpetual canon of praise.

Today's Christian worship and praise music is wonderful—a blessing to my heart. We should always be singing a new song to the Lord, and every generation needs to contribute to the vast body of our hymnody. I'm having a problem, however, retaining most of the newer songs in my long-term memory because they come and go like cars on a turnpike. Just as I become familiar with one, it's pushed aside by a newer one. None of them are settling into my lifelong personal treasure of worship because all of them are here today, gone tomorrow.

That truly isn't a criticism, because many of them have become dear to me. But somehow most of the newer songs are endearing but not enduring.

I'm also on a mission to save the great hymns of the faith that have outlasted the centuries and permeated the souls of one generation after another. We should know these hymns, teach them to our children, sing them in our churches, and treasure them in our devotions. The wonderful hymns in this prayer journal don't come and go like the latest style of jeans. They stay with us for a lifetime. They've blessed generations through the years, and because of their shelf life, their words have a way of lodging in our memories.

As long as we don't lose them.

A friend recently asked me why we should retain the hymns since methods of ministry change while the message does not. That's a great question. A modern praise song may have essentially the same message as "Amazing Grace," but in a more up-to-date mode. Why not discard the former and keep the latter?

Well, when Ezra was compiling the Hebrew hymnal—I'm almost certain it was Ezra who collected the psalms into the final arrangement we have in our Bibles—he included the most modern songs available (such as Psalm 126, written at the end of the Babylonian captivity about 539 BC) alongside much older hymns like Psalm 90, written by Moses nearly a thousand years before.

There's an ingenious philosophy behind that approach to worship, and it's reflected in the words of Jesus—truly wise people bring out of their storehouses treasures both new and old (Matthew 13:52). We need to stay anchored to the past while pressing into the future. If we lose our heritage, we'll simply float with the tides and trends and, likely as not, we'll end up in shallow waters.

The Bible tells us to sing "psalms and hymns and spiritual songs" (Ephesians 5:19). Biblical scholars have debated the differences among those terms, but it seems pretty clear to me. Psalms are words of Scripture put to music, especially from the Old Testament book of Psalms. Hymns are sturdy, objective, durable, lasting anthems of praise—the kind you'll find in this prayer journal. And spiritual songs are fresher, lighter, mostly subjective, and newer.

I speak in a lot of churches, and many congregations are obeying only one-third of this command. We have lots of "spiritual songs," and thank God for them. Still, let's not dismiss the psalms and hymns or relegate them to the nursing homes. I often tell congregations that older people badly need to sing newer music, and younger people badly need to sing the older hymns.

The classic without the contemporary is dated; the contemporary without the classic is detached. When you blend the two, you have something deep, durable, and divine.

On an encouraging note, the classic hymns have never been more accessible. I almost always have my online music tuned to the great hymns. I cherish them. I relish remembering their words. I'm uplifted when I hear the fabulous strains of "Be Thou My Vision," "Jesus Shall Reign," and "O Worship the King."

The songs we've known all our lives remain in our memories even when our memories begin to fade and the Lord initiates the process of taking us Home. And if there's a song in this prayer journal you don't know, congratulations! You have a new treasure to discover.

The focus of *Then Sings My Soul Prayer Journal* is . . . prayer. Most of the hymns you'll find within these covers are worded in the form of prayer, and how many times I've needed them! Some days when my soul is downcast and my prayers aren't forthcoming, I can listen to "Holy, Holy, Holy! Lord God Almighty," which is a prayer addressed to God, and pretty soon I'm singing along with the recording and my melancholy is broken. I've never failed to be moved by the stanza that says:

*Holy, holy, holy! Though the darkness hide Thee,*
*Though the eye of sinful man Thy glory may not see;*
*Only Thou art holy; there is none beside Thee,*
*Perfect in power, in love, and purity.*

"Take My Life and Let It Be" is Frances Havergal's great consecration hymn, and its stanzas cover every area of life. It's a wonderful prayer to pray as we daily rededicate ourselves to God.

Recently I've really started to appreciate "I Need Thee Every Hour." Sometimes as I walk from my home to my office, I find myself singing:

*I need Thee, O I need thee,*
*Ev'ry hour I need Thee!*
*O bless me now, my Savior,*
*I come to Thee!*

The truth is, I have a personal connection to all the hymns in this collection. I recall Ruth Bell Graham telling me that when nothing else would lift a cloud of discouragement from her mind, she would sing "Immortal, Invisible, God Only Wise."

I recall learning "Jesus, I Am Resting, Resting" while in college, and I bumped into it again in reading the biography of missionary Hudson Taylor. It was his favorite hymn, and the message behind that hymn changed his life and ministry.

The words of "All Creatures of Our God and King" thrilled me so much I traveled to the little town of Assisi to visit the place where St. Francis composed it.

About a month before Katrina passed away, we had a visit from a group of German church musicians, led by my friend Johannes Schroeder. Katrina had returned home from the hospital only the day before, so we had a meal catered on the patio. Afterward the group gathered around her and sang several great German hymns. I told them our favorite German hymn was "Praise Ye the Lord, the Almighty" by Joachim Neander. I still have the video of their voices filling the place, singing forth as my dear wife's face lit up like sunshine.

The hymns can do that. Mature Christians often look back over their lives and find certain hymns etched into their experiences at critical times. I recall my senior year in college, facing graduation without any idea what to do next. Some afternoons, I'd hike through the woods around our campus, singing, "Savior, Like a Shepherd Lead Me."

And He did.

As a young man, I worked in the Billy Graham crusades, and some of the most sacred moments in the museum of my memories involve Dr. Graham finishing his sermon and bowing his head as the choir sang, "Just As I Am Without One Plea." I watched night after night as hundreds of people filed toward the platform to receive Jesus as their Savior and Lord.

I recall my mother singing "What a Friend We Have in Jesus."

I recall my friend Tom Tipton singing "Precious Lord, Take My Hand."

Perhaps my favorite hymn in this collection is the great hymn of gratitude "Now Thank We All Our God." It's another German hymn, written during the Thirty Years' War (1618–1648). It's not familiar to a lot of people; but once you learn it, you'll never leave it. Just ponder the second verse with me a moment:

> *O may this bounteous God*
> *Through all our life be near us,*
> *With ever joyful hearts*
> *And blessed peace to cheer us,*
> *And keep us in His grace,*
> *And guide us when perplexed,*
> *And free us from all ills*
> *In this world and the next.*

Have you ever seen the word "perplexed" in a hymn or song? Yet how often do we feel perplexed? Whenever I'm confused about life, I turn to this great hymn and sing it as a prayer to Him who knows the way.

Here, then, are fifty-two hymns you can study, sing, pray, share, and add to your lifelong canon of praise. Let's encourage our churches to sing them, because we don't want to become the first generation since the Reformation to lose all that's come before us. The loss would be greater than we can endure. Except for the Bible, our hymnals provide the greatest treasure trove of theological and devotional material in existence anywhere.

Let's sing a new song to the Lord—without losing the old ones!

*Come, Thou Almighty King,*
*Help us Thy name to sing,*
*Help us to praise . . . !*

# Come, Thou Almighty King

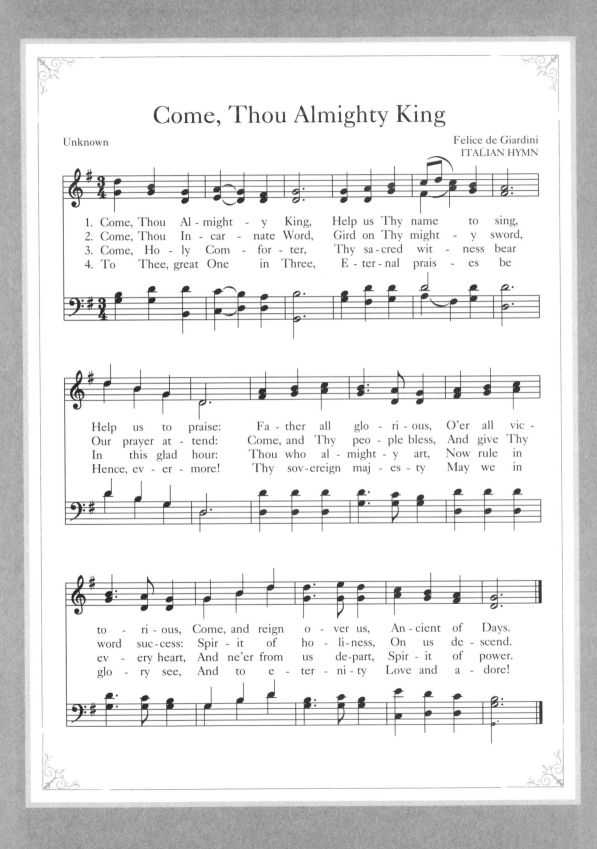

# COME, THOU ALMIGHTY KING

1757

This is one of our oldest English hymns, but its authorship is unknown. It was published in or before 1757, and one of the oldest imprints is in a four-page Methodist pamphlet. Some people have attributed it to Charles Wesley. But most hymnologists reject that attribution since it's written to a meter that Wesley never used and the great hymnist never claimed it as his own. A number of old sources speculate that the real author was Rev. Martin Madan (1726–1790), who was an English lawyer–turned–Methodist preacher with a reputation as a stirring orator and a gifted musician.

At first, this hymn was sung to the same tune as "God Save the King." On the American side of the Atlantic, we use the same tune for "My Country, 'Tis of Thee." Just as an experiment, try singing a verse of "Come, Thou Almighty King" to this slower, more somber melody. There's an interesting story connected with it. During the American Revolution, while British troops were occupying New York City and appeared to be winning the war, a group of English soldiers went to church one Sunday morning in Long Island. The setting was tense. The occupiers demanded the congregation sing "God Save the King" in honor of King George III. The organist was forced to begin playing the tune—but instead of singing "God Save the King," the congregation broke out in "Come, Thou *Almighty* King."[1]

Point made.

I don't remember *not* knowing this hymn. In the mountain church I attended in childhood, it was one of three songs that opened almost every Sunday morning service, the others being "Holy, Holy, Holy! Lord God Almighty" and "O Worship the King." I love those hymns to this day. After all, what better prayer can a church offer than: "Come, and Thy people bless, and give Thy word success"?

Since 1769, the majestic tune ITALIAN HYMN has been used as the musical setting for "Come, Thou Almighty King." It was composed by Felice de Giardini, the Italian composer and violinist.

"I have revealed and saved and proclaimed—
I, and not some foreign god among you.
You are my witnesses," declares the LORD, "that I am God.
Yes, and from ancient days I am he.
No one can deliver out of my hand.
When I act, who can reverse it?"
—ISAIAH 43:12–13 (NIV)

# REFLECT

. . . . . . . . . . . . . . . . . . . . . . . . . . . . . . . . . . . . . . .

We learn here that this hymn was sung in a nonviolent protest against British occupation during the American Revolution. How is God's royalty different from human royalty?

_____

_____

_____

_____

_____

The verses of this hymn highlight the three persons of the Trinity: Father, Son, and Holy Spirit, beginning with the Father in verse one. What does it mean to have a Father who is also a King?

_____

_____

_____

_____

_____

Verse two asks Christ to grant a "spirit of holiness." What would that look like?

_____

_____

_____

Verse three notes that the Holy Spirit is a "spirit of power." How have you experienced that power in your life?

_____

_____

_____

> _O Trinity, my all, You are the immensity in which I can lose myself, the Almighty Power to which I can surrender, the holy ground in which I can bury myself, the infinitely beautiful light which I can contemplate for all eternity. Amen._
>
> —ELISABETH CATEZ (1880–1906)

## PRAYER REQUESTS FOR THE WEEK

_____

_____

# God, Our Father, We Adore You

George W. Frazer
Alfred S. Loizeaux, st. 3

John Zundel
BEECHER

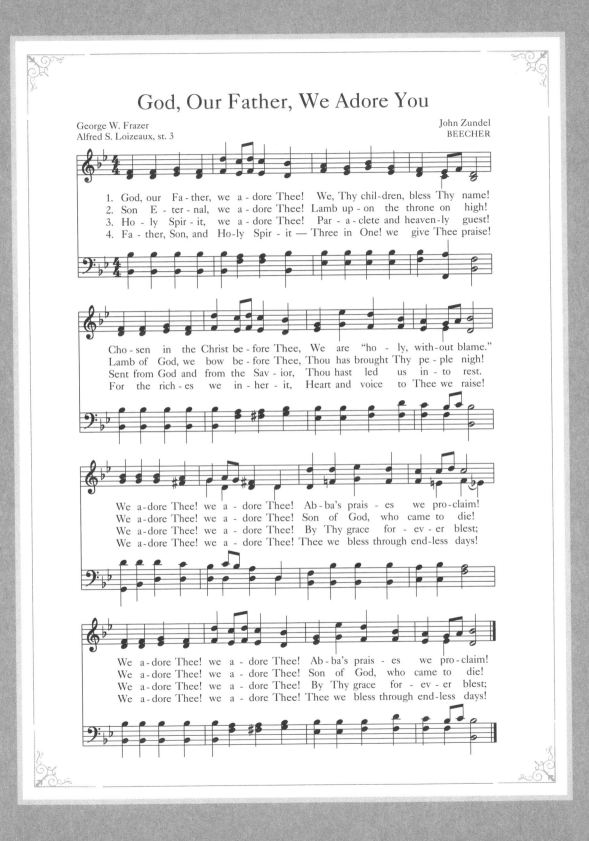

1. God, our Fa-ther, we a-dore Thee! We, Thy chil-dren, bless Thy name!
2. Son E-ter-nal, we a-dore Thee! Lamb up-on the throne on high!
3. Ho-ly Spir-it, we a-dore Thee! Par-a-clete and heaven-ly guest!
4. Fa-ther, Son, and Ho-ly Spir-it — Three in One! we give Thee praise!

Cho-sen in the Christ be-fore Thee, We are "ho-ly, with-out blame."
Lamb of God, we bow be-fore Thee, Thou has brought Thy pe-ple nigh!
Sent from God and from the Sav-ior, Thou hast led us in-to rest.
For the rich-es we in-her-it, Heart and voice to Thee we raise!

We a-dore Thee! we a-dore Thee! Ab-ba's prais-es we pro-claim!
We a-dore Thee! we a-dore Thee! Son of God, who came to die!
We a-dore Thee! we a-dore Thee! By Thy grace for-ev-er blest;
We a-dore Thee! we a-dore Thee! Thee we bless through end-less days!

We a-dore Thee! we a-dore Thee! Ab-ba's prais-es we pro-claim!
We a-dore Thee! we a-dore Thee! Son of God, who came to die!
We a-dore Thee! we a-dore Thee! By Thy grace for-ev-er blest;
We a-dore Thee! we a-dore Thee! Thee we bless through end-less days!

# GOD, OUR FATHER, WE ADORE THEE

1884

Georg Frazer, the twenty-year-old son of an Irish police inspector, was working in a Dublin bank when his older brother invited him to an evangelistic rally. The evangelist, Dr. H. Grattan Guinness, was drawing huge crowds in Dublin's Rotunda. George went with his brother but they were unable to get in because of the crowds. Climbing a guttering pipe, George viewed the service through an upper window. Dr. Guiness's sermon pierced his heart, and George struggled for two weeks before yielding his life to Christ. He continued working at the bank, but George was a new man. He reveled in sharing his faith with others. Soon he was engaged in personal and public evangelistic work. At length, he entered full-time ministry, moving to England and settling in the town of Cheltenham. There he published three volumes on hymns, *Midnight Praises, Day-Dawn Praises,* and *The Day Spring.*

His widely loved hymn on the Trinity, "God, Our Father, We Adore Thee," first appeared in *Midnight Praises* in 1884 and was published in the United States in 1904. (In 1952, Alfred Loizeaux replaced Frazer's original third verse with a revised stanza about the Holy Spirit.)

George Frazer was fifty-six when he passed away. "I grieve to leave my work for the Master . . . and all whom I love," he said, "but it is infinitely more precious to me to be with Christ than all besides." His tombstone says:

GEORGE WEST FRAZER

Departed to be with Christ

January 24, 1896, Aged 56

"THOU REMAINEST" (Heb. 1.11)

His spirit now has winged its way to those bright realms of cloudless day;

Then, mourner, cease to weep; for better is it thus to be

From self, the world, and Satan free, by Jesus put to sleep.

And, Thou, Lord, in the beginning hast laid the foundation of the earth; and the heavens are the works of thine hands: They shall perish; but thou remainest; and they all shall wax old as doth a garment.

—HEBREWS 1:10–11 (KJV)

# REFLECT

The words "Thou remainest" from Hebrews 1, featured on hymnist George Frazer's tombstone, seem to allude to Paul's words in 2 Corinthians 5:8. What does Paul say about being absent from the body?

Stanza one uses quotation marks when referring to Christians as "holy, without blame," referencing Ephesians 1:4. Is it easy or difficult for you to accept this description of yourself?

Stanza one refers to the Father as "Abba." Do you remember this term being used in Scripture? What does it mean to you?

_____

_____

_____

Stanza three (Alfred Loizeaux's addition) refers to the Holy Spirit as a "heavenly guest." Have you experienced this to be true? In what ways?

_____

_____

_____

> _O Lord, let me not henceforth desire health or life, except to spend them for You, with You, and in You. You alone know what is good for me; do, therefore, what seems best to You. Give to me, or take from me; conform my will to Yours; and grant that, with humble and perfect submission, and in holy confidence, I may receive the orders of Your eternal Providence; and may equally adore all that comes to me from You; through Jesus Christ our Lord. Amen._
>
> —BLAISE PASCAL (1623–1662)

## PRAYER REQUESTS FOR THE WEEK

_____

_____

# Shout to the Lord

Darlene Zschech

Darlene Zschech
Arr. by Eric Wyse
SHOUT TO THE LORD

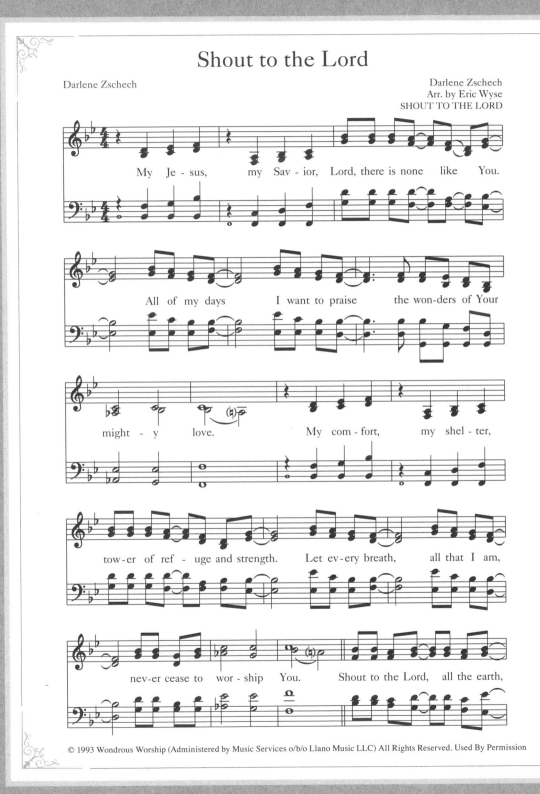

My Je-sus, my Sav-ior, Lord, there is none like You.

All of my days I want to praise the won-ders of Your

might-y love. My com-fort, my shel-ter,

tow-er of ref - uge and strength. Let ev-ery breath, all that I am,

nev-er cease to wor-ship You. Shout to the Lord, all the earth,

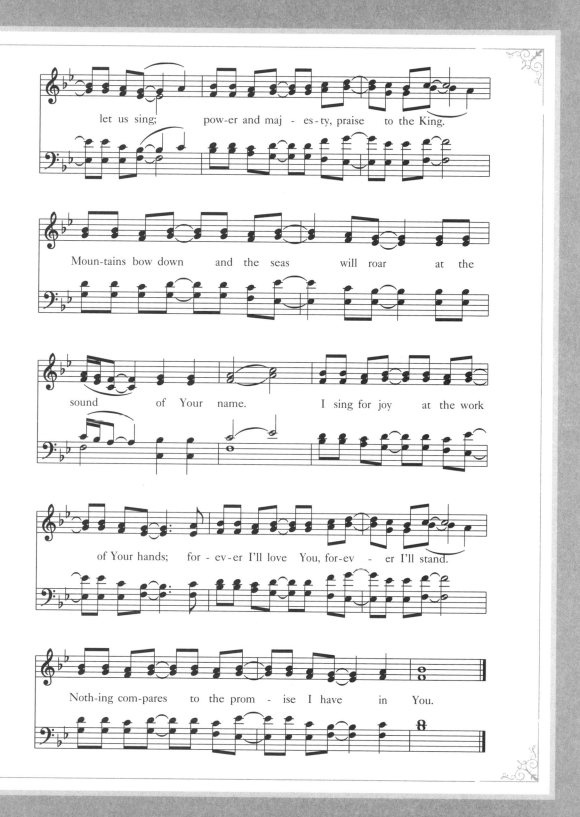

# SHOUT TO THE LORD

[ 1993 ]

The Bible contains promises for every problem and a word of assurance for every need. When faced with anger or anxiety, we can always find a word from God to nudge us onward and upward—if only we'll open His Book. That's what Darlene Zschech did one dark day in 1993.

Darlene was born in 1965 in Brisbane, Australia, and she grew up singing. When she was about fifteen, her father, who had recently given his life to Christ, enrolled her in a Christian scouting program; and through that program she received Jesus Christ as her Savior.

Years later, one day in 1993, Darlene faced a daunting and discouraging personal problem. In her heaviness, she entered the study of her home and sat at the old and out-of-tune piano her parents had given her when she was five. Opening her Bible, she started reading Psalm 96.

As Darlene meditated on that psalm, her fingers pressed the keys of the piano, and the music and words began to flow. In about twenty minutes the song was done. For several days she sang it to herself as the truths of the song ministered to her own heart. She had not previously called herself a songwriter, so Darlene was reluctant to share it with anyone. But mustering her courage, she finally asked the music pastor at her church to listen to it. She was so nervous she kept stopping and apologizing. She even asked him to stand over by the wall and turn away from her while she sang it.

He assured her the song was wonderful, and shortly afterward they sang "Shout to the Lord" during the offering at church. The congregation took to it quickly, standing and joining in the song, though the words hadn't been prepared for bulletin or screen. Darlene's pastor, Brian Houston, predicted it would be sung around the world.

And so it has.

# REFLECT

. . . . . . . . . . . . . . . . . . . . . . . . . . . . . . . . . . . . . . . . .

Darlene Zschech wrote "Shout to the Lord" while feeling discouraged and sad. How does singing it make you feel?

_____

_____

_____

_____

_____

The psalms inspired Zschech's lyrics, especially Psalm 96. What does Psalm 100:1 say?

_____

_____

_____

_____

_____

Consider this line: "All of my days / I want to praise." Desire ("want") often determines whether or not we praise God. What happens when you don't really want to, but you do it anyway?

---

What does Philippians 2:9–11 say about the sound of the name of Jesus?

---

> *Give ear to my words, O LORD,*
> *Consider my meditation.*
> *Give heed to the voice of my cry,*
> *My King and my God,*
> *For to You I will pray.*
> *My voice You shall hear in the morning, O LORD;*
> *In the morning I will direct it to You,*
> *And I will look up.*
>
> —PSALM 5:1–3 (NKJV)
>
> *Amen.*

## PRAYER REQUESTS FOR THE WEEK

# Commit Whatever Grieves Thee

Paul Gerhardt

Hans L. Hassler
Harm. by Johann Sebastian Bach
PASSION CHORALE

1. Com - mit what - ev - er grieves thee In - to the gra - cious hands
2. On Him place Thy re - li - ance If thou wouldst be se - cure;
3. Thy truth and grace, O Fa - ther, Most sure - ly see and know
4. Thy hand is nev - er short - ened, All things must serve Thy might;

Of Him who nev - er leaves thee, Who heaven and earth com - mands.
His work thou mus con - sid - er If thine is to en - dure.
Both what is good and e - vil For mor - tal man be - low.
Thine ev - ery act is bless - ing, Thy path is pur - est light.

Who points the clouds their cours - es, Whom winds and waves o - bey,
By anx - ious sighs and griev - ing And self - tor - ment - ing care
Ac - cord - ing to Thy coun - sel Thou wilt Thy work pur - sue;
Thy work no man can hin - der, Thy pur - pose none can stay,

He will di - rect thy foot - steps And find for thee a way.
God is not moved to giv - ing; All must be gained by prayer.
And what Thy wis - dom choos - eth Thy might will al - ways do.
Since Thou to bless Thy chil - dren Wilt al - ways find a way.

# COMMIT WHATEVER GRIEVES THEE

## 1656

The first stanza of this hymn is easy to memorize, and well worth the effort. In cadence and content, it flows as naturally as cascading water: "Commit whatever grieves thee into the gracious hands / Of Him who never leaves thee, who heaven and earth commands." I often quote it in sermons or counseling.

Paul Gerhardt knew what he was writing about. Considered Germany's greatest hymnist, he was a man whose whole life was encompassed by troubles. In 1618, while he was still a child, the Thirty Years' War broke out, and he lived much of his life amid its horrors. The University of Wittenberg remained open, and there Gerhardt studied for the ministry, greatly influenced by two professors who were lovers of Lutheran hymns.

Upon graduation, Gerhardt accepted a position as tutor for a family in Berlin, and later he began pastoring in the nearby town of Mittenwalde. There he wrote many of the hymns for which he is remembered. He later moved to Berlin and became the pastor of St. Nicholas Church. But this was a time of bickering between the Lutherans and the Reformed clergy, and the Elector Frederick William deposed Gerhardt from his position in 1666.

"This is only a small Berlin affliction," he said, "but I am also willing and ready to seal with my blood the evangelical truth, and like my namesake, St. Paul, to offer my neck to the sword."

Gerhardt's wife, it seems, didn't immediately share his stalwartness. According to an old story (impossible to confirm), as they left Berlin for parts unknown, she was fearful and fretful. That evening at an inn, she poured out her problems and bemoaned her hard lot. Gerhardt tried to comfort her by quoting Psalm 37:5: "Commit your way to the LORD, trust also in Him, and He shall bring it to pass." But she had trouble resting in that assurance.

Going outside, Gerhardt sat on a garden seat and there composed the words to "Commit Whatever Grieves Thee." That evening as he quoted the hymn to her, her fear subsided and she was able to cast her cares into the gracious hands of Him who never leaves us, whom heav'n and earth commands.

Commit your way to the LORD;
    trust in him and he will do this:
He will make your righteous reward shine like
the dawn,
    your vindication like the noonday sun.
    —PSALM 37:5–6 (NIV)

# REFLECT

How might the words of this hymn have been fortifying to Paul Gerhardt's wife?

_____

_____

_____

_____

_____

Paul Gerhardt drew inspiration for this hymn from Psalm 37:5. Read that passage and consider how you might "commit your way" to the Lord.

_____

_____

_____

_____

_____

What, if anything, is grieving you today? How might you commit it to God?

_____

_____

_____

What passage from Scripture might have inspired the line, "Since Thou to bless Thy children / Wilt always find a way"?

_____

_____

_____

> *Let me hold fast to You, beautiful Lord, whom the angels themselves yearn to look upon. Wherever You go, I will follow You. . . . You carry my griefs, because You grieve for my sake. You passed through the narrow doorway from death to life, to make it wide enough for all to follow. Nothing can ever now separate me from Your love. Amen.*
> —BERNARD OF CLAIRVAUX (1090–1153)

## PRAYER REQUESTS FOR THE WEEK

_____

_____

# Come, My Soul, Thy Suit Prepare

John Newton

Henri A. César Malan
HENDON

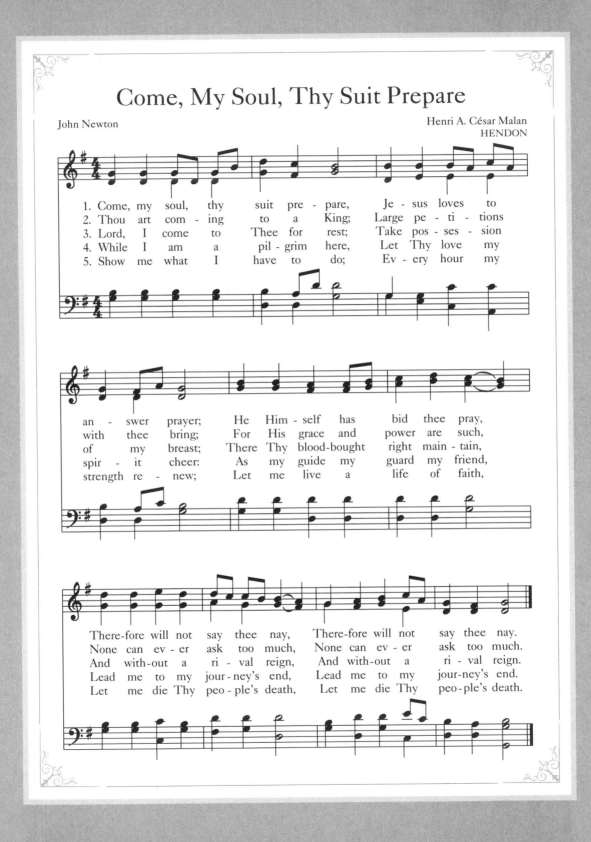

1. Come, my soul, thy suit pre - pare,
2. Thou art com - ing to a King;
3. Lord, I come to Thee for rest;
4. While I am a pil - grim here,
5. Show me what I have to do;

Je - sus loves to
Large pe - ti - tions
Take pos - ses - sion
Let Thy love my
Ev - ery hour my

an - swer prayer;
with thee bring;
of my breast;
spir - it cheer:
strength re - new;

He Him - self has bid thee pray,
For His grace and power are such,
There Thy blood-bought right main - tain,
As my guide my guard my friend,
Let me live a life of faith,

There-fore will not say thee nay,
None can ev - er ask too much,
And with-out a ri - val reign,
Lead me to my jour-ney's end,
Let me die Thy peo - ple's death,

There-fore will not say thee nay.
None can ev - er ask too much.
And with-out a ri - val reign.
Lead me to my jour-ney's end.
Let me die Thy peo-ple's death.

# COME, MY SOUL, THY SUIT PREPARE

### 1779

The author of this hymn is John Newton, whose story I've told in two previous volumes of *Then Sings My Soul*. He was the famous slave-trader who, following his conversion to Christ, became one of England's most celebrated preachers and the author of "Amazing Grace."

Newton's hymn "Come, My Soul, Thy Suit Prepare" deals with the subject of prayer, the word "suit" meaning "petition." It holds a special place in my memory because when I was in college, I had the privilege of spending time with Ruth (Mrs. Billy) Graham. In discussing prayer, she quoted the second verse of this hymn from memory and with a knowing smile: "Thou art coming to a King, / Large petitions with thee bring, / For His grace and power are such / None can ever ask too much."

Those words instantly engraved themselves on my mind in an unusual exercise of sudden memorization and I've often quoted them since.

"Come, My Soul, Thy Suit Prepare" originally appeared in *The Olney Hymns*, compiled by Newton and his troubled friend William Cowper. Newton was vicar in the village of Olney, England. Wanting to encourage Cowper, Newton drew him into a partnership of writing hymns for their church. The two men lived on parallel streets with an orchard between them. They paid the orchard owner a guinea a year for the right to pass through his land to their respective gardens. Here they spent many hours discussing Newton's sermons and their corresponding hymns. Cowper called the garden his "verse manufactory."

When *The Olney Hymns* was published in 1779, Cowper's name was attached to over sixty of them; Newton's to over 280. The hymnal was so popular that by 1836 there were thirty-seven official editions and many unauthorized editions. *The Olney Hymns* presented the evangelical truths of the Christian faith in both theological and personal verse.

## VERSE OF THE WEEK

Do not be anxious about anything, but in every situation, by prayer and petition, with thanksgiving, present your requests to God. And the peace of God, which transcends all understanding, will guard your hearts and your minds in Christ Jesus.

—Philippians 4:6–7 (niv)

## REFLECT

What world-famous hymn did John Newton write? Do you see any similarities between that one and "Come, My Soul, Thy Suit Prepare"?

_____

_____

_____

_____

_____

Consider the audacious claim of the second verse: "Thou art coming to a King, / Large petitions with thee bring, / For His grace and power are such / None can ever ask too much." Have you ever hesitated to bring something to God in prayer for fear it was too "large"?

_____

_____

_____

_____

Verse three notes that the author comes to God for "rest" and subsequently asks that God reign in his heart. How are rest and God's presence related?

_____

_____

_____

What does verse five mean by "Let me die Thy people's death"?

_____

_____

_____

> *Yours, O Lord, is the day, Yours also is the night; cover our sins with Your mercy as You cover the earth with darkness; and grant that the Son of Righteousness may always shine in our hearts, to chase away the darkness of all evil thoughts; through Jesus Christ our Lord. Amen.*
> —ANONYMOUS

## PRAYER REQUESTS FOR THE WEEK

_____

_____

# Be Thou My Vision

Irish Hymn, c. 8th Century                                    Irish Folk Melody

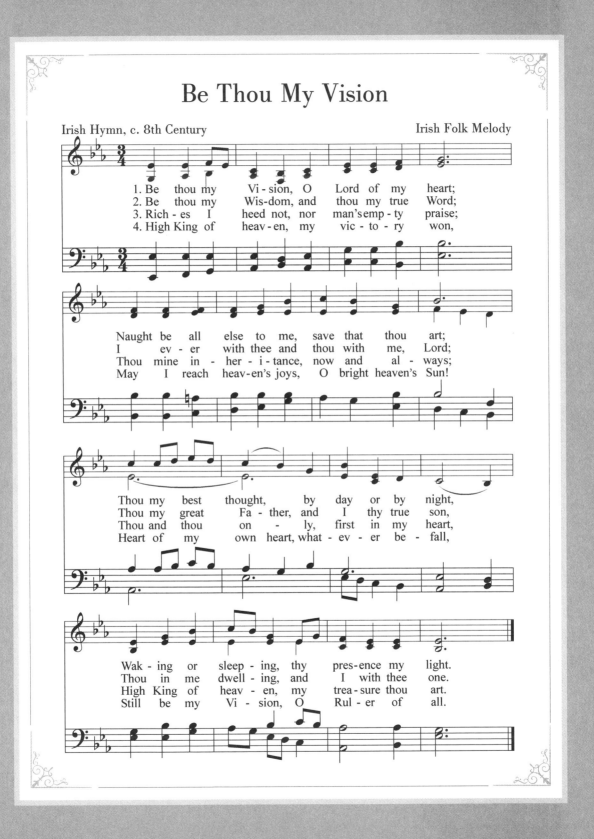

1. Be thou my Vi - sion, O Lord of my heart;
2. Be thou my Wis-dom, and thou my true Word;
3. Rich - es I heed not, nor man's emp - ty praise;
4. High King of heav - en, my vic - to - ry won,

Naught be all else to me, save that thou art;
I ev - er with thee and thou with me, Lord;
Thou mine in - her - i - tance, now and al - ways;
May I reach heav - en's joys, O bright heaven's Sun!

Thou my best thought, by day or by night,
Thou my great Fa - ther, and I thy true son,
Thou and thou on - ly, first in my heart,
Heart of my own heart, what - ev - er be - fall,

Wak - ing or sleep - ing, thy pres - ence my light.
Thou in me dwell - ing, and I with thee one.
High King of heav - en, my trea - sure thou art.
Still be my Vi - sion, O Rul - er of all.

# BE THOU MY VISION

Only one missionary is honored with a global holiday, and only one is known by his own distinct color of green—St. Patrick, of course, missionary to Ireland.

Patrick was born in AD 373 along the banks of the River Clyde in what is now called Scotland. His father was a deacon, and his grandfather a priest. When Patrick was about sixteen, raiders descended on his little town and torched his home. When one of the pirates spotted him in the bushes, he was seized, hauled aboard ship, and taken to Ireland as a slave. There he gave his life to the Lord Jesus.

"The Lord opened my mind to an awareness of my unbelief," he later wrote, "in order that I might remember my transgressions and turn with all my heart to the Lord my God."

Patrick eventually escaped and returned home. His overjoyed family begged him never to leave again. But one night, in a dream reminiscent of Paul's vision of the Macedonian man in Acts 16, Patrick saw an Irishman pleading with him to come evangelize Ireland.

It wasn't an easy decision, but Patrick, about thirty, returned to his former captors with only one book, the Latin Bible, in his hand. As he evangelized the countryside, multitudes came to listen. The superstitious Druids opposed him and sought his death. But his preaching was powerful, and Patrick became one of the most fruitful evangelists of all time, planting about 200 churches and baptizing 100,000 converts.

His work endured, and several centuries later, the Irish church was still producing hymns, prayers, sermons, and songs of worship. In the eighth century, an unknown poet wrote a prayer asking God to be his Vision, his Wisdom, and his Best Thought by day or night.

In 1905, Mary Elizabeth Byrne, a scholar in Dublin, Ireland, translated this ancient Irish poem into English. Another scholar, Eleanor Hull of Manchester, England, took Byrne's translation and crafted it into verses with rhyme and meter. Shortly thereafter it was set to a traditional Irish folk song, "Slane," named for an area in Ireland where Patrick reportedly challenged local Druids with the gospel.

It is one of our oldest and most moving hymns:

*Be Thou my vision, O Lord of my heart,*
*Naught be all else to me save that Thou art.*
*Thou my best thought by day or by night,*
*Waking or sleeping, Thy presence my light.*

Go therefore and make disciples of all the nations, baptizing them in the name of the Father and of the Son and of the Holy Spirit.

—Matthew 28:19

# REFLECT

As a young man, Patrick was enslaved by the Irish, then later willingly went as a missionary to the Irish. Have you ever been unjustly wronged? Have injustices hardened your heart? Consider whether there might be some injustice you need to forgive today.

The so-called Great Commission of Matthew 28:19 challenges believers to share the message of Jesus Christ. Patrick is an extreme example of living out that challenge. How can you fulfill that charge?

How is God your "best thought" (verse one)?

_____

_____

_____

Verse three of this hymn calls God's presence our "inheritance." How is a divine inheritance different from an earthly inheritance?

_____

_____

_____

> *As my head rests on my pillow, let my soul rest in Your mercy. As my limbs relax on my mattress, let my soul relax in Your peace. As my body finds warmth beneath blankets, let my soul find warmth in Your love. As my mind is filled with dreams, let my soul be filled with visions of Your Heaven. Amen.*
>
> —JOHANN FREYLINGHAUSEN (1670–1739)

## PRAYER REQUESTS FOR THE WEEK

_____

_____

# Fairest Lord Jesus

Anonymous German Hymn

*Schlesische Volkslieder* arr. by Richard S. Willis

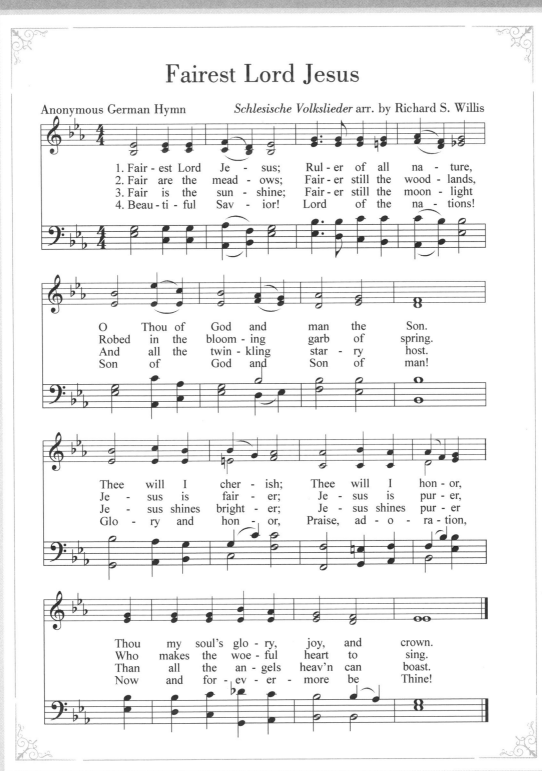

1. Fair - est Lord Je - sus; Rul - er of all na - ture,
2. Fair are the mead - ows; Fair - er still the wood - lands,
3. Fair is the sun - shine; Fair - er still the moon - light
4. Beau - ti - ful Sav - ior! Lord of the na - tions!

O Thou of God and man the Son.
Robed in the bloom - ing garb of spring.
And all the twin - kling star - ry host.
Son of God and Son of man!

Thee will I cher - ish; Thee will I hon - or,
Je - sus is fair - er; Je - sus is pur - er,
Je - sus shines bright - er; Je - sus shines pur - er
Glo - ry and hon - or, Praise, ad - o - ra - tion,

Thou my soul's glo - ry, joy, and crown.
Who makes the woe - ful heart to sing.
Than all the an - gels heav'n can boast.
Now and for - ev - er - more be Thine!

# FAIREST LORD JESUS

1677

This hymn came from Roman Catholic Jesuits in Germany and originally had six verses. It first appeared in 1677 in a Jesuit hymnbook titled *Münster Gesangbuch*, but the text of the hymn was in existence at least fifteen years earlier, for it has been found in a manuscript dating back to 1662. Yet the origin of the words remains a mystery.

Who translated it into English? That, too, is largely a mystery. The first three stanzas are the work of an anonymous translator. The fourth stanza was by Joseph A. Seiss, and it first appeared in a Lutheran Sunday school book in 1873.

How appropriate that no human author draws attention from the great theme of this song. There's no source to distract from the subject, no story to detract from the Savior.

This hymn emphasizes the beauty and wonder of Christ, and it alludes to His dual nature, that He was both human and divine, God made flesh, the God-Man: *O Thou of God and man the Son . . . Son of God and Son of Man!*

It brings to mind one of the greatest observations ever made about Christ, uttered by the "golden-mouthed" preacher of Antioch, John Chrysostom, in a fourth-century sermon: "I do not think of Christ as God alone, or man alone, but both together. For I know He was hungry, and I know that with five loaves He fed five thousand. I know He was thirsty, and I know that He turned the water into wine. I know He was carried in a ship, and I know that He walked on the sea. I know that He died, and I know that He raised the dead. I know that He was set before Pilate, and I know that He sits with the Father on His throne. I know that He was worshiped by angels, and I know that He was stoned by the Jews. And truly some of these I ascribe to the human, and others to the divine nature. For by reason of this He is said to have been both God and man."

*Beautiful Savior! Lord of the nations!*
*Son of God and Son of Man!*
*Glory and honor, praise, adoration,*
*Now and forevermore be Thine!*

For unto us a Child is born, unto us a Son is given. . . .
And His name will be called Wonderful, Counselor,
Mighty God, Everlasting Father, Prince of Peace.

—ISAIAH 9:6

# REFLECT

Isaiah 9:6, written centuries prior to the birth of Christ, proclaimed that the Messiah would be both "Child" and "Mighty God." While the two seemed to be opposite, both were true. Write about how that sits with you.

This hymn calls Jesus "fairest"—an antiquated word that we usually associate with princesses in fairy tales, but it can also mean gentle and peaceful. Does that word still resonate with you? Why or why not?

_____

_____

_____

_____

How can we "cherish" and "honor" Jesus as stated in the hymn?

_____

_____

_____

Verse three says Jesus' presence makes the "woeful heart to sing." Have you ever uttered the name of Jesus when you were in pain or sad? What effect does that have?

_____

_____

_____

> _O holy Jesus, meek Lamb of God; Bread that came down from heaven; light and life of all holy souls: help me to a true and living faith in You. Open Yourself within me with all Your holy nature and spirit, that I may be born again by You, and in You be a new creation, brought alive and revived, led and ruled by Your Holy Spirit. Amen._
> —WILLIAM LAW (1686–1761)

## PRAYER REQUESTS FOR THE WEEK

_____

_____

# O God, Our Help in Ages Past

Isaac Watts

William Croft

1. O God, our Help in ages past, Our
2. Un - der the sha - dow of Thy throne Still
3. Be - fore the hills in or - der stood, Or
4. A thou - sand a - ges in Thy sight, Are
5. Time like an ev - er roll - ing stream, Bears
6. O God, our Help in a - ges past, Our

Hope for years to come, Our Shel - ter from the
may we dwell se - cure; Suf - fi - cient is Thine
earth re - ceived her frame, From ev - er - last - ing
like an eve - ning gone; Short as the watch that
all its sons a - way; They fly, for - got - ten,
Hope for years to come, Be Thou my Guide while

storm - y blast, And our e - ter - nal Home!
arm a - lone, And our de - fense is sure.
Thou art God, To end - less years the same.
ends the night, Be - fore the ris - ing sun.
as a dream Dies at the open - ing day.
life shall last, And our e - ter - nal Home.

# O GOD, OUR HELP IN AGES PAST

1719

This hymn in Isaac Watts's 1719 *Psalms of David Imitated* is based on Psalm 90, and is perhaps Watts's most bracing hymn. It was played on the radio by the BBC as soon as World War II was declared and later was sung at the funeral service of Winston Churchill. Some of the original verses have fallen into disuse, but as you read them, think of the ailing hymnist, sitting at the desk in his room on the Abney estate, poring over Psalm 90 and penning these words:

> *O God, our help in ages past, / Our hope for years to come, /*
> *Our shelter from the stormy blast, / And our eternal home!*
> *Under the shadow of Thy throne / Thy saints have dwelt secure; /*
> *Sufficient is Thine arm alone, / And our defense is sure.*
> *Before the hills in order stood, / Or earth received her frame, /*
> *From everlasting Thou art God, / To endless years the same.*
> *Thy Word commands our flesh to dust, / "Return, ye sons of men": /*
> *All nations rose from earth at first, / And turn to earth again.*
> *A thousand ages in Thy sight / Are like an evening gone; /*
> *Short as the watch that ends the night / Before the rising sun.*
> *The busy tribes of flesh and blood, / With all their lives and cares, /*
> *Are carried downwards by the flood, / And lost in following years.*
> *Time, like an ever rolling stream, / Bears all its sons away; /*
> *They fly, forgotten, as a dream / Dies at the opening day.*
> *Like flowery fields the nations stand / Pleased with the morning light; /*
> *The flowers beneath the mower's hand / Lie withering ere 'tis night.*
> *Our God, our help in ages past, / Our hope for years to come, /*
> *Be Thou our guard while troubles last, / And our eternal home.*

P.S. We also have a great Christmas carol from this 1719 collection. As Watts studied Psalm 98, especially verses 4–9, he worded them this way: *Joy to the world, the Lord is come! Let earth receive her King!*

Lord, You have been our dwelling place in all generations.
Before the mountains were brought forth,
Or ever You had formed the earth and the world,
Even from everlasting to everlasting, You are God.

—Psalm 90:1–2

# REFLECT

Drawing on the words of the psalmist, Isaac Watts recalls the faithfulness and sovereignty of God in generations past—and before God had even formed the earth and world. How can remembering the past fortify us for the present?

This hymn refers to God as Help, Hope, Shelter, and Home. In what way is God all four of these things to you?

_____

_____

_____

_____

_____

_____

_____

_____

The fourth verse is devoted to God's perspective on time. In what ways is this an assurance to you?

_____

_____

The final words of this hymn refer to our "eternal Home." How does the hope of heaven apply to the present moment?

_____

_____

> *O God, the beginning and the end of all things, who art always the same, and whose years fail not, I . . . kneel in adoration before Thee, and offer Thee my deepest thanks for the fatherly care with which Thou hast watched over me during the past, for the many times Thou hast protected me from evils of soul and body, and for the numberless blessings both temporal and spiritual, which Thou hast showered upon me. May it please Thee to accept the homage of my grateful heart which I offer Thee in union with the infinite thanksgiving of Thy divine Son, our Lord Jesus Christ, who with Thee liveth and reigneth forever and ever. Amen.*
> —ANONYMOUS CATHOLIC PRAYER

## PRAYER REQUESTS FOR THE WEEK

_____

_____

# Come, Thou Fount of Every Blessing

Robert Robinson

Traditional American Melody

1. Come, Thou fount of ev-ery bless - ing, Tune my heart to sing Thy grace.
2. Here I raise my Eb - e - ne - zer; Hith - er by Thy help I come.
3. Oh, to grace how great a debt - or Dai - ly I'm con-strained to be!

Streams of mer - cy, nev - er ceas - ing, Call for songs of loud-est praise.
And I hope, by Thy good plea - sure, Safe - ly to ar - rive at home.
Let Thy grace, Lord, like a fet - ter, Bind my wan - d'ring heart to Thee:

Teach me some me - lo - dious son - net, Sung by flam-ing tongues a - bove.
Je - sus sought me when a stran - ger Wand'ring from the fold of God;
Prone to wan - der, Lord, I feel it, Prone to leave the God I love.

Praise the mount! I'm fixed up - on it, Mount of God's un - chang - ing love.
He, to res - cue me from dan - ger, In - ter - posed His pre - cious blood.
Here's my heart, Lord, take and seal it, Seal it for Thy courts a - bove.

# COME, THOU FOUNT OF EVERY BLESSING

1758

Robert Robinson had a rough beginning. His father died when he was young, and his mother, unable to control him, sent him to London to learn barbering. What he learned instead was drinking and gang life. When he was seventeen, he and his friends reportedly visited a fortune-teller. Relaxed by alcohol, they laughed as she tried to tell their futures. But something about the encounter bothered Robert, and that evening he suggested to his buddies they attend the evangelistic meeting being held by George Whitefield.

Whitefield was one of history's greatest preachers, with a voice that was part foghorn and part violin. That night he preached from Matthew 3:7: "But when he saw many of the Pharisees and Sadducees coming to his baptism, he said to them, 'Brood of vipers! Who warned you to flee from the wrath to come?'" Bursting into tears, Whitefield exclaimed, "Oh, my hearers! The wrath to come! The wrath to come!"

Robert immediately sobered up and sensed Whitefield was preaching directly to him. The preacher's words haunted him for nearly three years, until December 10, 1755, when he gave his heart to Christ.

Robert soon entered the ministry, and three years later at age twenty-three, while serving Calvinist Methodist Chapel in Norfolk, England, he wrote a hymn for his sermon on Pentecost Sunday. It was a prayer that the Holy Spirit flood into our hearts with His streams of mercy, enabling us to sing God's praises and remain faithful to Him. "Come, Thou Fount of Every Blessing" has been a favorite of the church since that day.

Robinson continued working for the Lord until 1790, when he was invited to Birmingham, England, to preach for Dr. Joseph Priestly, a noted Unitarian. There, on the morning of June 8, he was found dead at age fifty-four, having passed away quietly during the night.

Take a few moments to offer this hymn as a personal prayer, especially remembering those last insightful lines:

> *Let thy grace, Lord, like a fetter, bind my wand'ring heart to Thee.*
> *Prone to wander, Lord, I feel it, prone to leave the God I love;*
> *Here's my heart, Lord, take and seal it, seal it for Thy courts above.*

The Lord is not slack concerning His promise, as some count slackness, but is longsuffering toward us, not willing that any should perish but that all should come to repentance.

—2 PETER 3:9

# REFLECT

• • • • • • • • • • • • • • • • • • • • • • • • • • • • • • • • • • • •

How is the desire of God's heart expressed in 2 Peter 3:9 vividly realized in the story of Robert Robinson? How was Robinson a recipient of God's promise?

As the hymn says, God is the source of all blessings, since "every good and perfect gift is from above" (James 1:17 NIV). What good gifts has God given you?

_____

_____

_____

_____

_____

The author of the hymn imagines mercy coming from God in unending streams. Have you ever believed the lie that God's mercy can cease? How does it make you feel to know the truth: that God's mercies are without end?

_____

_____

The author confesses being "prone to wander" but notes he's bound to God by grace like a "fetter." Have you ever felt prone to wander? What brought you back to God?

_____

_____

> *Blessed are Thou, O Lord, God of our fathers, that didst create changes of days and nights, that hast delivered us from the evil of this day, that has bestowed on us occasions of joy in the evening to get us through the night fearlessly in hope: for Thou art our light, salvation and strength of life—of whom then shall we be afraid? Glory be to Thee, O Lord, glory be to Thee, for all Thy divine perfections, for Thine inexpressible and unimaginable goodness and mercy. . . . Glory and praise and blessing and thanksgiving by the voices and concert of voices as well of angels as of men, and of all Thy saints in heaven, and of all Thy creation withal on earth. Amen.*
> —LANCELOT ANDREWES (1555–1626)

## PRAYER REQUESTS FOR THE WEEK

_____

_____

# Rock of Ages

Augustus M. Toplady

Thomas Hastings

1. Rock of A - ges, cleft for me, Let me
2. Could my tears for - ev - er flow? Could my
3. While I draw this fleet - ing breath, When my

hide my - self in Thee. Let the wa - ter and the
zeal no lan - guor know? These for sin could not a -
eyes shall close in death, When I rise to worlds un -

blood, From Thy wound - ed side which flowed, Be of
tone; Thou must save, and Thou a - lone. In my
known, And be - hold Thee on Thy throne, Rock of

sin the dou - ble cure, Save from wrath and make me pure.
hand no price I bring; Sim - ply to Thy cross I cling.
A - ges cleft for me, Let me hide my - self in Thee.

# ROCK OF AGES

1776

On November 4, 1740, a baby in Farnham, England, was given the formidable name of Augustus Montague Toplady. His father died in a war, his mother spoiled him, his friends thought him "sick and neurotic," and his relatives disliked him.

But Augustus was interested in the Lord. "I am now arrived at the age of eleven years," he wrote on his birthday. "I praise God I can remember no dreadful crime; to the Lord be the glory." By age twelve he was preaching sermons to whoever would listen. At fourteen he began writing hymns. At sixteen he was soundly converted to Christ while attending a service in a barn. And at twenty-two he was ordained an Anglican priest.

As a staunch Calvinist, he despised John Wesley's Arminian theology and bitterly attacked the great Methodist leader. "I believe him to be the most rancorous hater of the gospel-system that ever appeared on this island," Augustus wrote.

"Wesley is guilty of satanic shamelessness," he said on another occasion, "of acting the ignoble part of a lurking, shy assassin."

In 1776 Augustus wrote an article about God's forgiveness, intending it as a slap at Wesley. He ended his article with an original poem:

*Rock of Ages, cleft for me,*
*Let me hide myself in Thee.*
*Let the water and the blood,*
*From Thy wounded side which flowed,*
*Be of sin the double cure,*
*Save from wrath and make me pure.*

Augustus Toplady died at age thirty-eight, but his poem outlived him and has been called "the best known, best loved, and most widely useful" hymn in the English language. Oddly, it is remarkably similar to something Wesley had written thirty years before in the preface of a book of hymns for the Lord's Supper: "O Rock of Salvation, Rock struck and cleft for me, let those two Streams of Blood and Water which gushed from thy side, bring down Pardon and Holiness into my soul."

Perhaps the two men were not as incompatible as they thought.[2]

## VERSE OF THE WEEK

My Father, who has given them to Me, is greater than all;
and no one is able to snatch them out of My Father's hand.

—JOHN 10:29

# REFLECT

Jesus' words in John 10:29 assure us that we're safe in God's care. What image does Jesus evoke to illustrate that loving care?

_____

_____

_____

_____

_____

The author of the lyrics to this iconic hymn seemed not to be well-liked as a child, and he died at a relatively young age. In what way has his legacy outlived him?

_____

_____

_____

_____

God is depicted in this hymn as a rock where we can safely hide from threats. Have you ever felt comforted by the safety of God's presence? How does it make you feel to know that comfort is ours for the asking, even when we're not under threat?

_____

_____

Verse two says, "In my hand no price I bring." What do the final words of this verse imply is the payment for salvation?

_____

_____

_____

> *And now, O blessed Redeemer, my rock, my hope, and only sure defence, to Thee do I cheerfully commit both my soul and body. If Thy wise providence see fit, grant that I may rise in the morning, refreshed with sleep, and with a spirit of activity for the duties of the day, but whether I wake here or in eternity grant that my trust in Thee may remain sure, and my hope unshaken, through Jesus Christ our Lord. Amen.*
> —HENRY KIRKE WHITE (1785–1806)

## PRAYER REQUESTS FOR THE WEEK

_____

_____

# Holy, Holy, Holy! Lord God Almighty

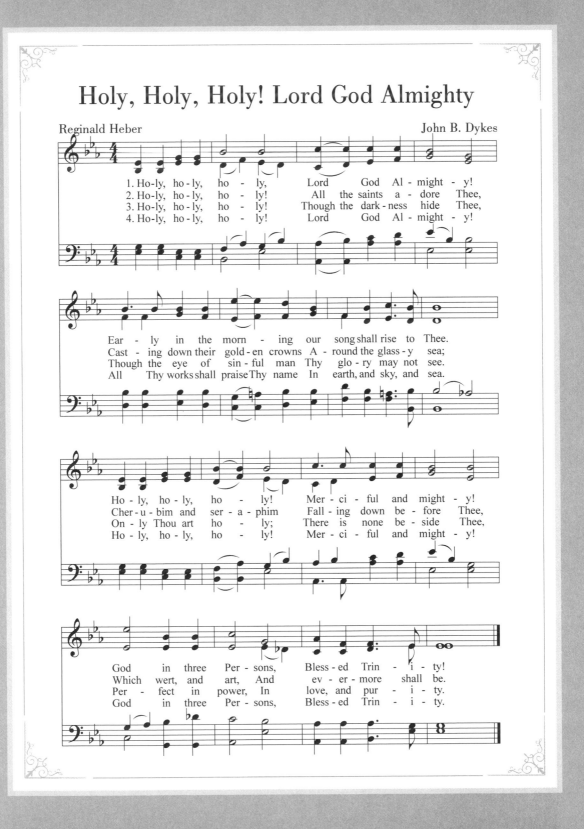

# HOLY, HOLY, HOLY! LORD GOD ALMIGHTY

1826

Reginald Heber was born April 21, 1783, to a minister and his wife in an English village. After a happy childhood and a good education in the village school, he enrolled at Oxford where he excelled in poetry and became fast friends with Sir Walter Scott. Following graduation, he succeeded his father as vicar in his family's parish, and for sixteen years he faithfully served his flock.

His bent toward poetry naturally gave him a keen and growing interest in hymnody. He sought to lift the literary quality of hymns, and he also dreamed of publishing a collection of high-caliber hymns corresponding to the church year for use by liturgical churches. But the Bishop of London wouldn't go along with it, and Heber's plans were disappointed.

He continued writing hymns for his own church, however, and it was during the sixteen years in the obscure parish of Hodnet that Heber wrote all fifty-seven of his hymns, including the great missionary hymn "From Greenland's Icy Mountains," which exhorted missionaries to take the gospel to faraway places like "Greenland's icy mountains" and "India's coral strand."

*From Greenland's icy mountains, / From India's coral strand, /*
*Where Afric's sunny fountains / Roll down their golden sand; /*
*From many an ancient river, / From many a palmy plain, /*
*They call us to deliver / Their land from error's chain.*

This hymn represented an earnest desire for Reginald, for he felt God was calling him as a missionary to "India's coral strand." His desire was fulfilled in 1822, when at age forty he was appointed to oversee the Church of England's ministries in India.

Arriving in Calcutta, he set out on a sixteen-month tour of his diocese, visiting mission stations across India. In February of 1826, he left for another tour. While in the village of Trichinopoly on April 3, 1826, he preached to a large crowd in the hot sun, and afterward plunged into a pool of cool water. He suffered a stroke and drowned.

It was after his death that his widow, finding his fifty-seven hymns in a trunk, succeeded in publishing his *Hymns Written and Adapted to the Weekly Service of the Church Year*. In this volume was the great Trinitarian hymn based on Revelation 4:8–11, "Holy, Holy, Holy! Lord God Almighty."

## VERSE OF THE WEEK

And they do not rest day or night, saying: "Holy, holy, holy, Lord God Almighty, who was and is and is to come!"

—REVELATION 4:8

# REFLECT

. . . . . . . . . . . . . . . . . . . . . . . . . . . . . . . . . . . . . . . . . . . . .

Reginald Heber died tragically after proclaiming the gospel to a large audience. How do you think he would like to be remembered for this hymn?

_____

_____

_____

_____

_____

The repetition of the word "holy" in this hymn echoes Revelation 4:8. Do you think there's significance to the number three? Why or why not?

_____

_____

_____

_____

_____

The hymn evokes the sense of praising God in heaven with phrases like "casting down their golden crowns / Around the glassy sea." What imagery in the lyrics stands out most to you?

_____

_____

The song notes that all God's "works" shall praise His name. What have you seen today that seems to praise God?

_____

_____

_____

> *Worthy of praise from every mouth, of confession from every tongue, of worship from every creature, is Thy glorious name, O Father, Son, and Holy Ghost: who didst create the world in Thy grace and by Thy compassion didst save the world. To Thy majesty, O God, ten thousand times ten thousand bow down and adore, singing and praising without ceasing and saying, Holy, holy, holy, Lord God of hosts; Heaven and earth are full of Thy praises; Hosanna in the highest. Amen.*
>
> —NESTORIAN LITURGY (5TH C.)

## PRAYER REQUESTS FOR THE WEEK

_____

_____

# I Need Thee Every Hour

Annie S. Hawks; Robert Lowry, Refrain

Robert Lowry

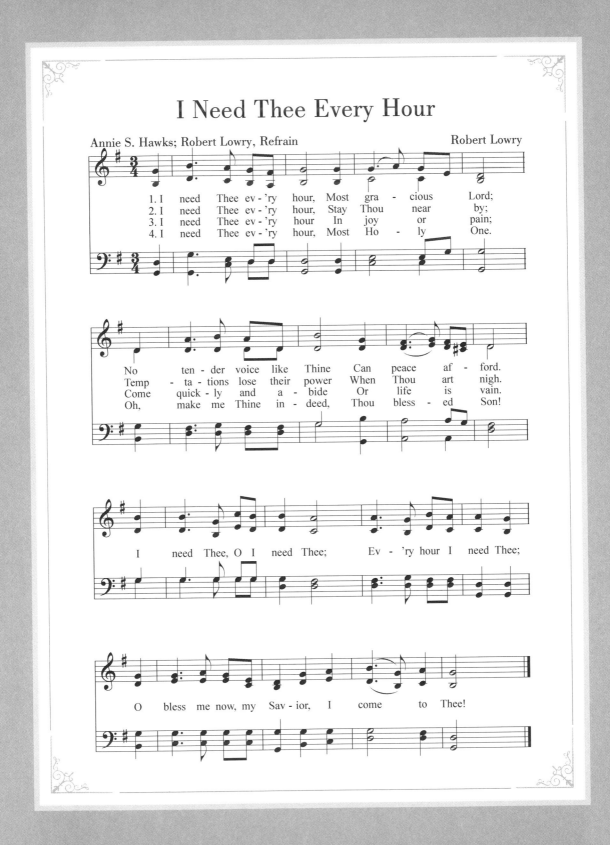

1. I need Thee ev - 'ry hour, Most gra - cious Lord;
2. I need Thee ev - 'ry hour, Stay Thou near by;
3. I need Thee ev - 'ry hour, In joy or pain;
4. I need Thee ev - 'ry hour, Most Ho - ly One.

No ten - der voice like Thine Can peace af - ford.
Temp - ta - tions lose their power When Thou art nigh.
Come quick - ly and a - bide Or life is vain.
Oh, make me Thine in - deed, Thou bless - ed Son!

I need Thee, O I need Thee; Ev - 'ry hour I need Thee;

O bless me now, my Sav - ior, I come to Thee!

# I NEED THEE EVERY HOUR

1872

In his book *The Practice of the Presence of God*, Brother Lawrence claimed to be as close to God while working in the kitchen as when praying in the chapel. The Lord, after all, is always near us, thus wherever we are is holy ground. That was the experience of Annie Hawks, a housewife and mother of three in Brooklyn, New York.

As a child, Annie Sherwood had dabbled in poetry, her first verse being published when she was fourteen. In 1857, she married Charles Hawks and they established their home in Brooklyn, joining Dr. Robert Lowry's Hanson Place Baptist Church. With the good doctor's encouragement, she began writing Sunday school songs for children, and he set many of them to music.

"I Need Thee Every Hour" was written on a bright June morning in 1872. Annie later wrote, "One day as a young wife and mother of thirty-seven years of age, I was busy with my regular household tasks. Suddenly, I became so filled with the sense of nearness to the Master that, wondering how one could live without Him, either in joy or pain, these words, 'I Need Thee Every Hour,' were ushered into my mind, the thought at once taking full possession of me."

The next Sunday, Annie handed these words to Dr. Lowry, who wrote the tune and chorus while seated at the little organ in the living room of his Brooklyn parsonage. Later that year, it was sung for the first time at the National Baptist Sunday School Association meeting in Cincinnati, Ohio, and published in a hymnbook the following year.

When Annie's husband died sixteen years later, she found that her own hymn was among her greatest comforts. "I did not understand at first why this hymn had touched the great throbbing heart of humanity," Annie wrote. "It was not until long after, when the shadow fell over my way, the shadow of a great loss, that I understood something of the comforting power in the words which I had been permitted to give out to others in my hour of sweet serenity and peace."

Sometime after Charles's death, Annie moved to Bennington, Vermont, to live with her daughter and son-in-law. All in all, she wrote over 400 hymns during her eighty-three years, though only this one is still widely sung.

Not that we are sufficient of ourselves to think of anything as being from ourselves, but our sufficiency is from God.

—2 CORINTHIANS 3:5

# REFLECT

· · · · · · · · · · · · · · · · · · · · · · · · · · · · · · · · · · · · · · · · · ·

Of the four hundred hymns written by Annie S. Hawks, most have been forgotten, yet this one is still widely sung. Why do you think it still resonates with believers?

_____

_____

_____

_____

Consider the line "No tender voice like Thine / Can peace afford." How does God's presence affect you when you're anxious or afraid?

_____

_____

_____

_____

Do you find that "temptations lose their power" when God is near? Is that something you desire? Why or why not?

_____

_____

_____

Second Corinthians 3:5 points out that our "sufficiency" is from God. Do you cling to self-reliance? Is there an aspect of that you'd like to let go of today?

_____

_____

_____

> *Eternal God, who committest to us the swift and solemn trust of life; since I know not what a day may bring forth, but only that the hour for serving Thee is always present, may I wake to the instant claims of Thy holy will; not waiting for tomorrow, but yielding today. In all things draw me to the mind of Christ, that . . . Thou mayest own me as at one with Him and Thee. Amen.*
>
> —JAMES MARTINEAU (1805–1900)

## PRAYER REQUESTS FOR THE WEEK

_____

_____

# Take My Life and Let It Be

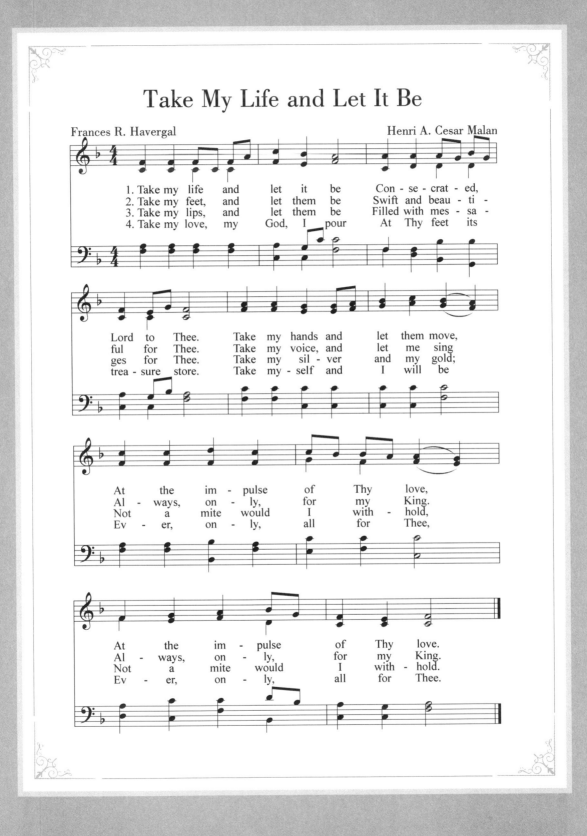

# TAKE MY LIFE AND LET IT BE

## 1874

Although hymnist Frances Havergal, thirty-six, had served the Lord for years, she felt something was missing in her Christian experience. Then one day in 1873, she received a little book called *All for Jesus*, which stressed the importance of making Christ the King of every corner and cubicle of one's life. Soon thereafter, she made a fresh and complete consecration of herself to Christ.

Years later when asked about it, she replied, "Yes, it was on Advent Sunday, December 2, 1873, I first saw clearly the blessedness of true consecration. I saw it as a flash of electric light, and what you see you can never un-see. There must be full surrender before there can be full blessedness."

Not long afterward, she found herself spending several days with ten people in a house, some of them unconverted. Others were Christians, but not fully surrendered to Christ. "Lord, give me all in this house," she prayed. She went to work witnessing, and before she left, all ten were yielded Christians. On the last night of her visit, Frances—too excited to sleep—wrote this great consecration hymn, "Take My Life and Let It Be."

In the years that followed, Frances frequently used this hymn in her own devotions, especially every December 2, on the anniversary of her consecration.

On one occasion, as she pondered the words, "Take my voice and let me sing / Always, only, for my King," she felt she should give up her secular concerts. Her beautiful voice was in demand, and she frequently sang with the Philharmonic. But from that moment, her lips were exclusively devoted to the songs of the Lord.

On another occasion she was praying over the stanza that says, "Take my silver and my gold; / Not a mite would I withhold." She had accumulated a great deal of jewelry, but she now felt she should donate it to the Church Missionary Society. Writing to a friend, she said, "I retain only a brooch for daily wear, which is a memorial to my dear parents; also a locket with the holy portrait I have of my niece in heaven. Evelyn, I had no idea I had such a jeweler's shop; nearly fifty articles are being packed off. I don't think I need to tell you I never packed a box with such pleasure."

Have you given your whole life—everything—over to Jesus? Why not make this the date of your own complete consecration?

Yet indeed I also count all things loss for the excellence of the knowledge of Christ Jesus my Lord, for whom I have suffered the loss of all things, and count them as rubbish, that I may gain Christ.

—PHILIPPIANS 3:8

# REFLECT

What book inspired Frances R. Havergal to consecrate her life to Christ? What are some of the books that have enriched your faith journey?

The word "consecrated" indicates a separate and special use. How might life be different if you "consecrated" your hands, feet, and voice to God?

_____

_____

_____

_____

_____

Is there something you've neglected to surrender to God? Will you offer it to Him today?

_____

_____

Philippians 3:8 says that through having lost, Paul "gained" Christ. Have you ever lost something special only to discover something more valuable?

_____

_____

_____

> _Thou hast made me, O Lord, when I was not, and that according to Thine own image. Thou from the very first instant of my being has been my God, my Father, my Deliverer, and all my good. Thou, with the benefits of Thy providence, hast preserved my life even till this present. O, let it be spent in Thy service! But because these things, O gracious Lord, cost Thee nothing, to bind me more fast to Thee, Thou wouldst need give me a present bought by Thee most dearly. Thou hast come down from heaven, to seek me in all those ways in which I had lost myself. O, draw up my soul unto Thee! Amen._
>
> —Augustine Baker (1575–1641)

## PRAYER REQUESTS FOR THE WEEK

_____

_____

# Have Thine Own Way, Lord

Adelaide A. Pollard

George C. Stebbins

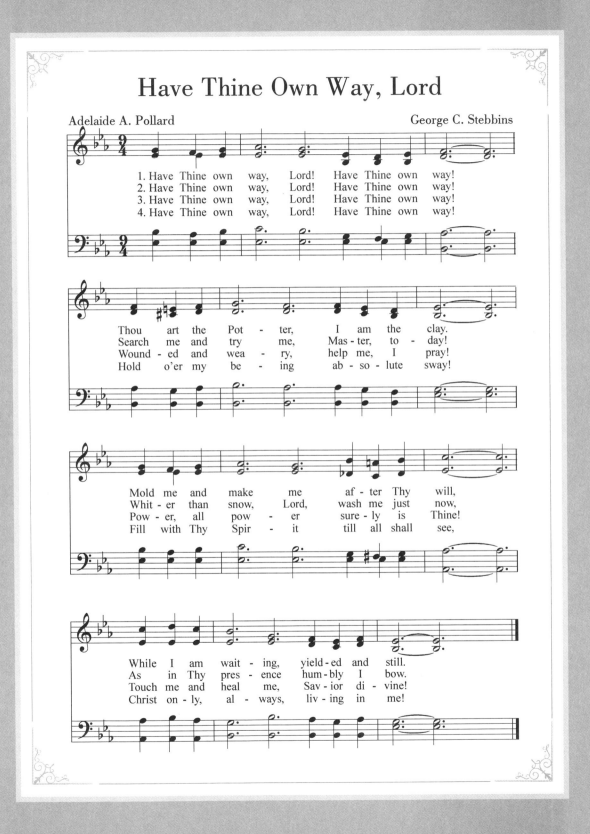

1. Have Thine own way, Lord! Have Thine own way!
2. Have Thine own way, Lord! Have Thine own way!
3. Have Thine own way, Lord! Have Thine own way!
4. Have Thine own way, Lord! Have Thine own way!

Thou art the Pot - ter, I am the clay.
Search me and try me, Mas - ter, to - day!
Wound - ed and wea - ry, help me, I pray!
Hold o'er my be - ing ab - so - lute sway!

Mold me and make me af - ter Thy will,
Whit - er than snow, Lord, wash me just now,
Pow - er, all pow - er sure - ly is Thine!
Fill with Thy Spir - it till all shall see,

While I am wait - ing, yield - ed and still.
As in Thy pres - ence hum - bly I bow.
Touch me and heal me, Sav - ior di - vine!
Christ on - ly, al - ways, liv - ing in me!

# HAVE THINE OWN WAY, LORD

1907

Hope deferred makes the heart sick," says Proverbs 13:12. Yet "*dis*appointments are *His* appointments." God uses setbacks to renew our focus on Him, to strengthen our faith, and to divert us to other opportunities. In this case, a bitter disappointment led to one of our greatest invitational hymns.

Its author, Adelaide Pollard, was born in Iowa during the Civil War. Her parents named her Sarah, but when she was old enough, she changed her name to "Adelaide," not liking the name "Sarah." After attending the Boston School of Oratory (Emerson College), she moved to Chicago to teach in a girls' school.

While in Chicago and struggling with frail health, she was attracted to the strange ministry of John Alexander Dowie, a Scottish-born faith healer who was drawing international attention. In 1901, Dowie announced he was the Elijah who would precede the coming of Christ. Purchasing 6,800 acres of land outside Chicago, he began building "Zion City," which, despite a strong start, ended in failure. Adelaide, however, was apparently healed of diabetes through Dowie's ministry.

Afterward, she became very involved in the work of an evangelist named Sanford, who was predicting the imminent return of Christ. In New England, where she had moved to assist Sanford, she felt God was calling her to Africa as a missionary. But to her intense disappointment, she was unable to raise her financial support. Heartsick, Adelaide, in her forties at the time, attended a prayer meeting. That night an elderly woman prayed, "It doesn't matter what You bring into our lives, Lord. Just have Your own way with us."

That phrase rushed into Adelaide's heart, and the verses began shaping in her mind. At home that evening, she read again the story of the potter and the clay in Jeremiah 18. By bedtime she had written out the prayer "Have Thine Own Way."

Adelaide did eventually make it to Africa, but the outbreak of World War I sent her to Scotland and, later, back to America where she wrote poems, spoke to groups, and ministered freely.

In the middle of December 1934, Adelaide, seventy-two, purchased a ticket at New York's Penn Station. She was heading to Pennsylvania for a speaking engagement. While waiting for the train, she was stricken with a seizure and shortly thereafter died.

## VERSE OF THE WEEK

As the clay is in the potter's hand, so are you in
My hand.

—JEREMIAH 18:6

# REFLECT

The author of this hymn changed her given name to "Adelaide." Considering her life's many disappointments, what do you think this reveals about her personality?

_____

_____

_____

_____

_____

The essence of this hymn is complete surrender. When you read the lyrics, do you feel resistance—or relief?

_____

_____

_____

_____

_____

What does the fourth verse say will happen when the writer is filled with the Holy Spirit?

_____

_____

_____

Read Jeremiah 18:6. How does this promise of God's sovereignty make you feel?

_____

_____

_____

> *Glory to Thee, my God, this night for all the blessings of the light; keep me, O keep me, King of Kings, beneath Thine own almighty wings. Forgive me, Lord, for Thy dear Son, the ill that I this day have done, that with the world, myself, and Thee I, ere I sleep, at peace may be. Teach me to live, that I may dread the grave as little as my bed; teach me to die, that so I may triumphing rise at the last day. . . . Praise God, from whom all blessings flow; praise Him, all creatures here below; praise Him above, ye heavenly host; praise Father, Son, and Holy Ghost. Amen.*
> —BISHOP THOMAS KEN (1637–1711)

## PRAYER REQUESTS FOR THE WEEK

_____

_____

# Just As I Am

Charlotte Elliott

William B. Bradbury

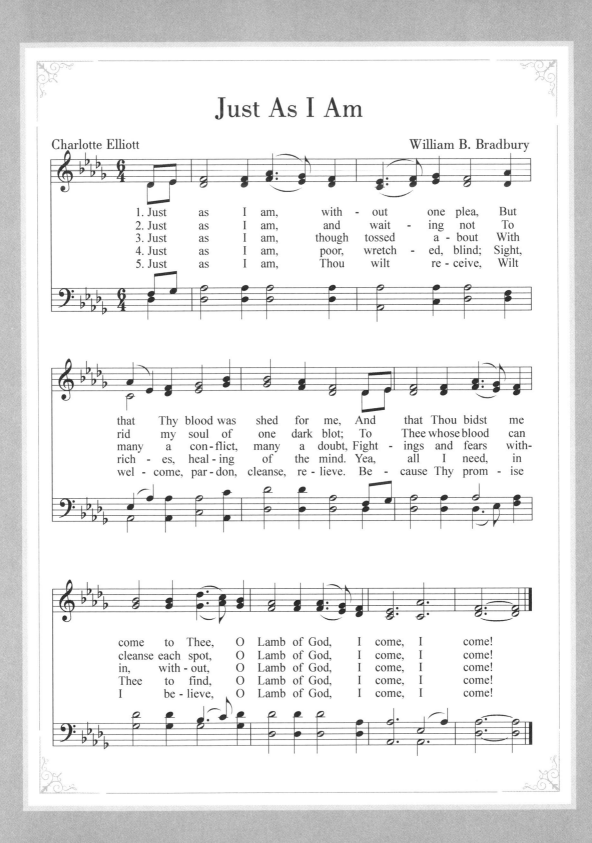

1. Just as I am, with-out one plea, But
2. Just as I am, and wait-ing not To
3. Just as I am, though tossed a-bout With
4. Just as I am, poor, wretch-ed, blind; Sight,
5. Just as I am, Thou wilt re-ceive, Wilt

that Thy blood was shed for me, And
rid my soul of one dark blot; To
many a con-flict, many a doubt, Fight-
rich - es, heal-ing of the mind. Yea,
wel - come, par-don, cleanse, re-lieve. Be-

that Thou bidst me
Thee whose blood can
ings and fears with-
all I need, in
cause Thy prom - ise

come to Thee, O Lamb of God, I come, I come!
cleanse each spot, O Lamb of God, I come, I come!
in, with - out, O Lamb of God, I come, I come!
Thee to find, O Lamb of God, I come, I come!
I be - lieve, O Lamb of God, I come, I come!

# JUST AS I AM

She was an embittered woman, Charlotte Elliott of Brighton, England. Her health was broken, and her disability had hardened her. "If God loved me," she muttered, "He would not have treated me this way."

Hoping to help her, a Swiss minister, Dr. Cesar Malan, visited the Elliotts on May 9, 1822. Over dinner, Charlotte lost her temper and railed against God and family in a violent outburst. Her embarrassed family left the room, and Dr. Malan was left alone with her.

"You are tired of yourself, aren't you?" he asked. "You are holding to your hate and anger because you have nothing else in the world to cling to. Consequently, you have become sour, bitter, and resentful."

"What is your cure?" asked Charlotte.

"The faith you are trying to despise."

As they talked, Charlotte softened. "If I wanted to become a Christian and to share the peace and joy you possess," she finally asked, "what would I do?"

"You would give yourself to God just as you are now, with your fightings and fears, hates and loves, pride and shame."

"I would come to God just as I am? Is that right?"

Charlotte did come just as she was, and her heart was changed that day. As time passed she found and claimed John 6:37 as a special verse for her: ". . . he who comes to Me I will by no means cast out."

Years later, her brother, Rev. Henry Elliott, was raising funds for a school for the children of poor clergymen. Charlotte wrote a poem, and it was printed and sold across England. The leaflet said: *Sold for the Benefit of St. Margaret's Hall, Brighton: Him That Cometh to Me I Will in No Wise Cast Out.* Underneath was Charlotte's poem—which has since become the most famous invitational hymn in history.

Charlotte lived to be eighty-two and wrote about 150 hymns, though she never enjoyed good health. As her loved ones sifted through her papers after her death, they found over a thousand letters she had kept in which people expressed their gratitude for the way this hymn had touched their lives.

All that the Father gives Me will come to Me, and the one who comes to Me I will by no means cast out.

—John 6:37

# REFLECT

· · · · · · · · · · · · · · · · · · · · · · · · · · · · · · · · · · · · · · · · ·

Often we believe we need to be cleaned up and sin-free to be accepted by God. On the contrary, this hymn reminds us that all we need to do is come as we are. What keeps you from thinking you are worthy of God's love?

_____

_____

_____

_____

Read John 6:37. What does this promise mean to you?

_____

_____

_____

_____

_____

Verse four presents the needs (poor, wretched, blind) in contrast to the blessings (sight, riches, healing of the mind). What requests do you have for the Lamb of God today?

_____

_____

"I come" is repeated at the end of each line of this song. In what ways are you in motion and on your way toward God's presence?

_____

_____

> *Lord, You have passed over into new life, and You now invite us to pass over also. In these past days we have grieved at Your suffering and mourned at Your death. We have given ourselves over to repentance and prayer, to abstinence and gravity. Now at Easter You tell us that we have died to sin. Yet, if this is so, how can we remain on earth? How can we pass over to Your risen life, while we are still in this world? Will we not be just as meddlesome, just as lazy, just as selfish as before? Will we not still be bad-tempered and stubborn, enmeshed in all the vices of the past? I pray that as we pass over with You, our faces will never look back. Instead, let us, like You, make Heaven on earth. Amen.*
>
> —BERNARD OF CLAIRVAUX (1090–1153)

## PRAYER REQUESTS FOR THE WEEK

_____

_____

# Joyful, Joyful, We Adore Thee

# JOYFUL, JOYFUL, WE ADORE THEE

1907

Once when recovering from a bout of depression, I found this hymn very therapeutic. "Melt the clouds of sin and sadness; drive the dark of doubt away," it says. "Giver of immortal gladness, fill us [me] with the light of day!" Notice how every phrase of this prayer is bursting with exuberance: The Lord is our "wellspring of the joy of living," our "ocean depth of happy rest," and we ask Him to "lift us to the joy divine."

The author of the hymn, Henry Jackson van Dyke, was born in Pennsylvania in 1852 and became pastor of the Brick Presbyterian Church in New York City. Henry later became professor of English literature at Princeton and the author of a number of books, including the still popular *The Other Wise Man*. He went on to occupy a number of eminent positions, including:

- American ambassador to the Netherlands and Luxembourg (appointed by his friend Woodrow Wilson)
- Lieutenant commander in the United States Navy Chaplains Corps during World War I
- Moderator of the General Assembly of the Presbyterian Church
- Commander of the Legion of Honor
- President of the National Institute of Arts and Letters
- Chairman of the committee that compiled the Presbyterian *Book of Common Worship*

In 1907, Henry van Dyke was invited to preach at Williams College in Massachusetts. At breakfast one morning, he handed the college president a piece of paper, saying, "Here is a hymn for you. Your mountains (the Berkshires) were my inspiration. It must be sung to the music of Beethoven's 'Hymn of Joy.'"

When he was later asked about his hymn, van Dyke replied: "These verses are simple expressions of common Christian feelings and desires in this present time—hymns of today that may be sung together by people who know the thought of the age, and are not afraid that any truth of science will destroy religion, or any revolution on earth overthrow the kingdom of heaven. Therefore this is a hymn of trust and joy and hope."

## VERSE OF THE WEEK

For I know the thoughts that I think toward you, says
the LORD, thoughts of peace and not of evil, to give
you a future and a hope.

—JEREMIAH 29:11

# REFLECT

What does it mean to "adore" God? How
do the words of this song show adoration?

How might "hearts unfold like flowers"
before God? Can you relate to this line?

_____

_____

_____

_____

_____

_____

_____

_____

_____

_____

Henry van Dyke found inspiration for this hymn in nature, delighting in the wonders of creation. How does nature inspire you to give God glory?

_____

_____

_____

Do you think the promise of Jeremiah 29:11 is about the present or the future? In what way does this encourage you?

_____

_____

_____

> *I adore, I venerate, I glory in that cross, which You represent to us, and by that cross I adore our merciful Lord, and what He has in mercy done for us! . . . By You, hell is spoiled; its mouth is closed to the redeemed. By You, demons are afraid, restrained and defeated. By You, the whole world is renewed and made beautiful. Amen.*
> —ANSELM OF CANTERBURY (1033–1109)

## PRAYER REQUESTS FOR THE WEEK

_____

_____

# How Great Thou Art

Carl Boberg

Swedish Folk Melody

1. O Lord, my God, When I in awe-some won-der, Con-sid-er
2. When thru the woods and for-est glades I wan-der, And hear the
3. And when I think that God, His Son not spar-ing, Sent Him to
4. When Christ shall come With shout of ac-cla-ma-tion And take me

all the worlds Thy hands have made; I see the stars, I hear the roll-ing
birds sing sweet-ly in the trees; When I look down from loft-y moun-tain
die, I scarce can take it in; That on the cross my bur-den glad-ly
home, What joy shall fill my heart! Then I shall bow In hum-ble ad-o-

thun-der, Thy pow'r through-out The u-ni-verse dis-played.
gran-deur And hear the brook and feel the gent-le breeze.
bear-ing, He bled and died To take a-way my sin.
ra-tion, And there pro-claim, "My God, how great Thou art!"

Then sings my soul, My Sav-ior God, to Thee, How great Thou art! How great Thou art!

Then sings my soul, My Sav-ior God, to Thee, How great Thou art! How great Thou art!

# HOW GREAT THOU ART

1885

Carl Boberg, a twenty-six-year-old Swedish minister, wrote a poem in 1885 that he called "O Store Gud"—"O Mighty God." The words, literally translated to English, said:

*When I the world consider, / Which Thou has made by Thine almighty Word, / And*
*how the web of life Thou wisdom guideth / And all creaion feedeth at Thy board.*
*Then doth my soul burst forth in song of praise, / Oh, great God! Oh, great God!*

His poem was published and "forgotten"—or so he thought. Several years later, Carl was surprised to hear it being sung to the tune of an old Swedish melody; but the poem and hymn did not achieve widespread fame.

Hearing this hymn in Russia, English missionary Stuart Hine was so moved he modified and expanded the words and made his own arrangement of the Swedish melody. He later said his first three verses were inspired, line upon line, by Russia's rugged Carpathian Mountains. The first verse was composed when he was caught in a thunderstorm in a Carpathian village, the second as he heard the birds sing near the Romanian border, and the third as he witnessed many of the Carpathian mountain-dwellers coming to Christ. The final verse was written after Dr. Hine returned to Great Britain.

Some time later, Dr. J. Edwin Orr[3] heard "How Great Thou Art" being sung by Naga tribes-people in Assam, in India, and decided to bring it back to America for use in his own meetings. When he introduced it at a conference in California, it came to the attention of music publisher Tim Spencer, who contacted Mr. Hine and had the song copyrighted. It was published and recorded.

During the 1954 Billy Graham Crusade in Harringay Arena, George Beverly Shea was given a leaflet containing this hymn. He sang it to himself and shared it with other members of the Graham team. Though not used in London, it was introduced the following year to audiences in Toronto.

In the New York Crusade of 1957, it was sung by Bev Shea ninety-nine times, with the choir joining the majestic refrain:

*Then sings my soul, my Savior God, to Thee,*
*How great Thou art! How great Thou art!*

For thus says the LORD, who created the heavens, who is God, who formed the earth and made it, who has established it, who did not create it in vain, who formed it to be inhabited: "I am the LORD, and there is no other."

—ISAIAH 45:18

# REFLECT

What does it mean for a soul to "sing"?

_____

_____

_____

_____

_____

_____

The first verse of this hymn focuses on the heavens—the marvels of the stars and the weather. When was the last time you "surveyed" the skies? What feelings did it evoke?

_____

_____

_____

_____

_____

Isaiah 48:15 reminds believers that God created the world and all that's in it. We humans often think we're in control, but God is sovereign. Is that a humbling or reassuring message? Why and how?

_____

_____

_____

In verse three, author Carl Boberg writes of Jesus' death, "I scarce can take it in." Take a moment to reflect on the horror and the exquisite beauty of the Cross.

_____

_____

_____

> *Great, O Lord, is Your kingdom, Your power, and Your glory; great also is Your wisdom, Your goodness, Your justice, Your mercy; and for all these we bless You, and will magnify Your name for ever and ever. Amen.*
> —GEORGE WITHER (1588–1667)

## PRAYER REQUESTS FOR THE WEEK

_____

_____

# Great Is Thy Faithfulness

Thomas O. Chisholm

William M. Runyan

1. Great is Thy faith - ful - ness, O God my Fa - ther,
2. Sum - mer and win - ter And spring - time and har - vest,
3. Par - don for sin And a peace that en - dur - eth,

There is no shad - ow Of turn - ing with Thee;
Sun, moon and stars In their cours - es a - bove;
Thine own dear pres - ence To cheer and to guide;

Thou chang - est not, Thy com - pas - sions they fail not;
Join with all na - ture In man - i - fold wit - ness
Strength for to - day And bright hope for to - mor - row,

As Thou hast been Thou for - ev - er wilt be.
To Thy great faith - ful - ness, Mer - cy and love.
Bless - ings all mine, With ten thou - sand be - side!

# GREAT IS THY FAITHFULNESS

### 1923

The author of this hymn, Thomas Obadiah Chisholm, was born in a log cabin in Kentucky. At age sixteen, he began teaching school, despite the paucity of his own education. He came to Christ at age twenty-seven under the ministry of evangelist H. C. Morrison. But Chisholm's health was unstable, and he alternated between bouts of illness and gainful employment in which he did everything from journalism to insurance to evangelistic work. Through all the ups and downs, he discovered new blessings from God every morning. The third chapter of Lamentations became precious to him: "His compassions fail not. They are new every morning; great is Your faithfulness" (Lamentations 3:22–23).

Thomas later admitted there was no dramatic story behind the writing of "Great Is Thy Faithfulness." While serving the Lord in Vincland, New Jersey, Thomas sent several poems to his friend, musician William Runyan, who was so moved by this one that he prayed earnestly for special guidance in composing the music. Runyan was in Baldwin, Kansas, at the time, and the hymn was published in 1923 in Runyan's private song pamphlets.

"It went rather slowly for several years," Thomas recalled. Then Dr. Will Houghton of the Moody Bible Institute of Chicago discovered it, and would say in chapel, "Well, I think we shall have to sing 'Great Is Thy Faithfulness.'" It became an unofficial theme song for the Institute; and when Houghton died, it was sung at his funeral.

Still, it remained relatively unknown until popularized around the world by George Beverly Shea and the choirs at the Billy Graham Crusades.

Thomas spent his retirement years in a Methodist Home for the Aged in Ocean Park, New Jersey, where he was frequently seen walking by the ocean and along town streets. Tom Rich, a resident of Ocean Park, recalls his pleasant demeanor as he dropped by the diner, sat on park benches, and fellowshipped with friends at Ocean Park's summer Bible conferences.

Thomas died in Ocean Park in 1960. During his lifetime he wrote twelve hundred poems and hymns. In addition to "Great Is Thy Faithfulness," he is the author of the well-known "O to Be Like Thee," as well as the hymn "Living for Jesus."

*Living for Jesus, a life that is true,*
*Striving to please Him in all that I do;*
*Yielding allegiance, glad hearted and free,*
*This is the pathway of blessing for me.*

Your mercy, O LORD, is in the heavens; your faithfulness reaches to the clouds.

—PSALM 36:5

# REFLECT

· · · · · · · · · · · · · · · · · · · · · · · · · · · · · · · · · · · ·

In a verse dedicated to God's unchanging nature we sing, "There is no shadow / Of turning with Thee; / Thou changest not, / Thy compassions they fail not." How is this assurance a gift in your life?

_____

_____

_____

_____

The author drew strength from Lamentations 3:22–23. How is God's compassion "new every morning"?

_____

_____

_____

_____

The lines of verse two talk about the seasons. How have the seasons of your life testified to God's faithfulness?

_____

_____

_____

What imagery does the psalmist use to illustrate God's faithfulness in Psalm 36:5?

_____

_____

_____

> *O God, Thou art the life of all who live, the light of the faithful, the strength of all who labor, and the repose of those who sleep in Christ. I thank Thee for the timely blessings of the day, and humbly beseech Thy merciful protection all the night. Bring me, I pray Thee, in safety to the morning hours, when I shall praise Thee again; through Him who died for us and rose again. Amen.*
> —*BOOK OF COMMON PRAYER* (1928)[4]

## PRAYER REQUESTS FOR THE WEEK

_____

_____

# I Am Thine, O Lord

Fanny J. Crosby

William H. Doane

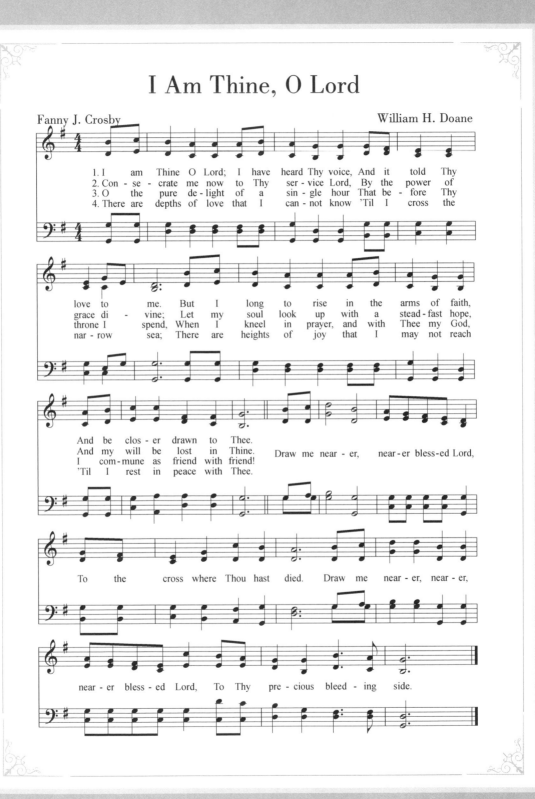

1. I am Thine O Lord; I have heard Thy voice, And it told Thy
2. Con - se - crate me now to Thy ser - vice Lord, By the power of
3. O the pure de - light of a sin - gle hour That be - fore Thy
4. There are depths of love that I can - not know 'Til I cross the

love to me. But I long to rise in the arms of faith,
grace di - vine; Let my soul look up with a stead - fast hope,
throne I spend, When I kneel in prayer, and with Thee my God,
nar - row sea; There are heights of joy that I may not reach

And be clos - er drawn to Thee.
And my will be lost in Thine. Draw me near - er, near - er bless - ed Lord,
I com - mune as friend with friend!
'Til I rest in peace with Thee.

To the cross where Thou hast died. Draw me near - er, near - er,

near - er bless - ed Lord, To Thy pre - cious bleed - ing side.

# I AM THINE, O LORD

### 1875

She's called the "Queen of American Hymnwriters," and the "Mother of Congregational Singing in America." During her ninety-five years, Fanny Crosby wrote more than eight thousand hymns. In addition, she was one of the three most prominent evangelical leaders in America during the last part of the 1800s, the others being D. L. Moody and Ira Sankey. She was one of America's most popular preachers and lecturers; in many cases lines of people would circle the block where she was scheduled to speak, hoping to get a seat.

When she traveled, it was usually by train; and she was fiercely independent, insisting on traveling alone, despite her blindness, until she was up in her eighties. Fanny lived in the run-down tenements of lower Manhattan so she'd be nearer her beloved rescue missions where she worked with the homeless and addicted.

But to me, the most remarkable thing about Fanny Crosby was her phenomenal memory. After her eyes were blinded in infancy, her grandmother Eunice took a special interest in teaching her Bible verses. Later a woman named Mrs. Hawley, the Crosbys' landlady, took over the job, committed to helping Fanny memorize the entire Bible! Every week, the child was given a certain number of chapters to learn, and Mrs. Hawley drilled them into her during their review sessions together. Fanny learned by heart all of Genesis, Exodus, Leviticus, Numbers, and Deuteronomy, plus the four Gospels, most of Psalms, all of Proverbs, and many portions of the rest of the Bible.

From the fountainhead of these Scriptures flowed her hymns.

Ira Sankey, in his autobiography, gives us the story behind this particular hymn: "Fanny Crosby was visiting Mr. W. H. Doane, in his home in Cincinnati, Ohio. They were talking together about the nearness of God, as the sun was setting and evening shadows were gathering around them. The subject so impressed the well-known hymnwriter that before retiring she had written the words to this hymn, which has become one of the most useful she has ever written. The music by Mr. Doane so well fitted the words that the hymn has become a special favorite wherever the gospel hymns are known."

It was first published in 1875 in the little hidden treasure of hymns called *Brightest and Best*. Underneath the hymn was this Scripture quotation: "Let us draw near with a true heart" (Hebrews 10:22).

Let us draw near with a true heart in full assurance of faith.

—HEBREWS 10:22

# REFLECT

· · · · · · · · · · · · · · · · · · · · · · · · · · · · · · · · · · · · · ·

Verse one refers to the Lord's "voice" telling of His love. In what way have you heard God's assurances of love?

_____

_____

_____

_____

_____

How do you think Fanny Crosby's blindness influenced the words of this hymn?

_____

_____

_____

_____

_____

Notice the words of the refrain, asking to be brought closer to Jesus on the cross. How would such nearness affect you?

_____

_____

_____

When this hymn was first published, it was paired with Hebrews 10:22. What does it mean to have a "true heart"?

_____

_____

_____

*Into Thine arms I now commend myself this night. I will lay me down in peace, if Thou speak peace to me through Jesus Christ. May my last thoughts be of Thee. And when I awake, may Thy Spirit bring heavenly things to my mind. Pardon the imperfections of my prayers. Supply what I have omitted to ask for, and do for me exceeding abundantly above all that I ask or think; for the merits of Jesus Christ our Lord. Amen.*
—F. FIELDING OULD (19TH C.)

## PRAYER REQUESTS FOR THE WEEK

_____

_____

# Now Thank We All Our God

Martin Rinkart

Johann Crüger

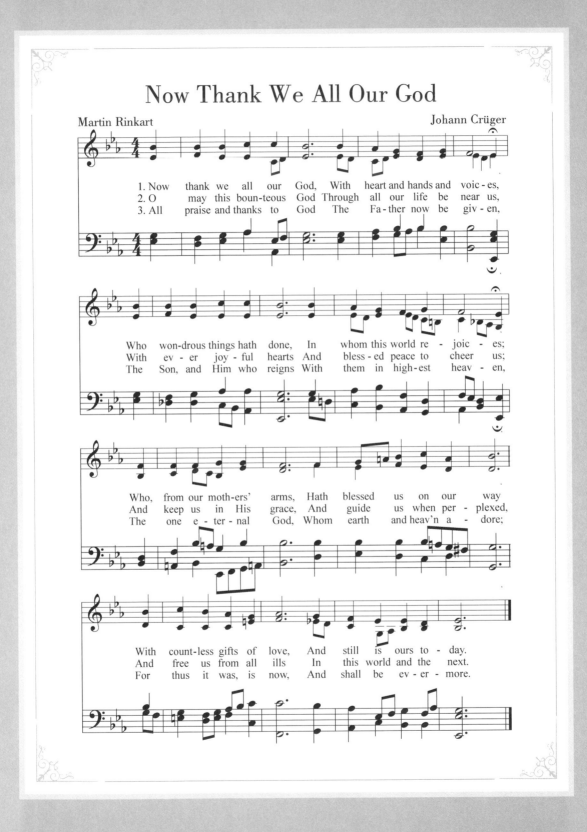

1. Now thank we all our God, With heart and hands and voic - es,
2. O may this boun-teous God Through all our life be near us,
3. All praise and thanks to God The Fa - ther now be giv - en,

Who won-drous things hath done, In whom this world re - joic - es;
With ev - er joy - ful hearts And bless - ed peace to cheer us;
The Son, and Him who reigns With them in high-est heav - en,

Who, from our moth-ers' arms, Hath blessed us on our way
And keep us in His grace, And guide us when per - plexed,
The one e - ter - nal God, Whom earth and heav'n a - dore;

With count-less gifts of love, And still is ours to - day.
And free us from all ills In this world and the next.
For thus it was, is now, And shall be ev - er - more.

# NOW THANK WE ALL OUR GOD

1636

An old English preacher once said, "A grateful mind is a great mind," and the Bible agrees. There are 138 passages of Scripture on the subject of thanksgiving, and some of them are powerfully worded. Colossians 3:17 says: "And whatever you do in word or deed, do all in the name of the Lord Jesus, giving thanks to God the Father through Him." First Thessalonians 5:18 adds, "In everything give thanks; for this is the will of God in Christ Jesus for you."

Unfortunately, few hymns are devoted exclusively to thanking God. Among the small, rich handful we do have is "Now Thank We All Our God." The German Christians sing this hymn like American believers sing the "Doxology," yet it's loved on both sides of the Atlantic and around the world.

It was written by Martin Rinkart (1586–1649), a Lutheran pastor in the little village of Eilenberg, Saxony. He grew up as the son of a poor coppersmith, felt called to the ministry, and after his theological training began his pastoral work just as the Thirty Years' War was raging through Germany.

Floods of refugees streamed into the walled city of Eilenberg. It was the most desperate of times. The Swedish army encompassed the city gates, and inside the walls there was nothing but plague, famine, and fear. Eight hundred homes were destroyed, and people began dying in increasing numbers. There was a tremendous strain on the pastors, who expended all their strength in preaching the gospel, caring for the sick and dying, and burying the dead. One after another, the pastors themselves took ill and perished until at last only Martin Rinkart was left. Some days he conducted as many as fifty funerals.

Finally the Swedes demanded a huge ransom. It was Martin Rinkart who left the safety of the city walls to negotiate with the enemy, and he did it with such courage and faith that there was soon a conclusion of hostilities, and the period of suffering ended.

Rinkart, knowing there is no healing without thanksgiving, composed this hymn for the survivors of Eilenberg. It has been sung around the world ever since.

*Now thank we all our God, / With heart and hands and voices,*
*Who wondrous things hath done, / In whom this world rejoices.*

## VERSE OF THE WEEK

In everything give thanks; for this is the will of God in Christ Jesus for you.

—1 Thessalonians 5:18

# REFLECT

Why do you suppose 138 passages of Scripture are dedicated to thanksgiving?

_____

_____

_____

_____

_____

The author of this hymn suffered through extremely dire circumstances. How do trials affect one's ability to give thanks?

_____

_____

_____

_____

_____

What are the three ways we give thanks cited in verse one?

_____

_____

_____

What does 1 Thessalonians 5:18 say about gratitude?

_____

_____

_____

> *Almighty God in Trinity, from all my heart be thanks to Thee for Thy good deed, that Thou me wrought, and with Thy precious blood me bought, and for all good Thou lendst to me, O Lord God, blessed may Thou be! All honour, joy and all loving be to Thy name without ending. Amen.*
> —RICHARD ROLLE (c. 1300–1349)

## PRAYER REQUESTS FOR THE WEEK

_____

_____

# Eternal Father, Strong to Save

William Whiting

John B. Dykes

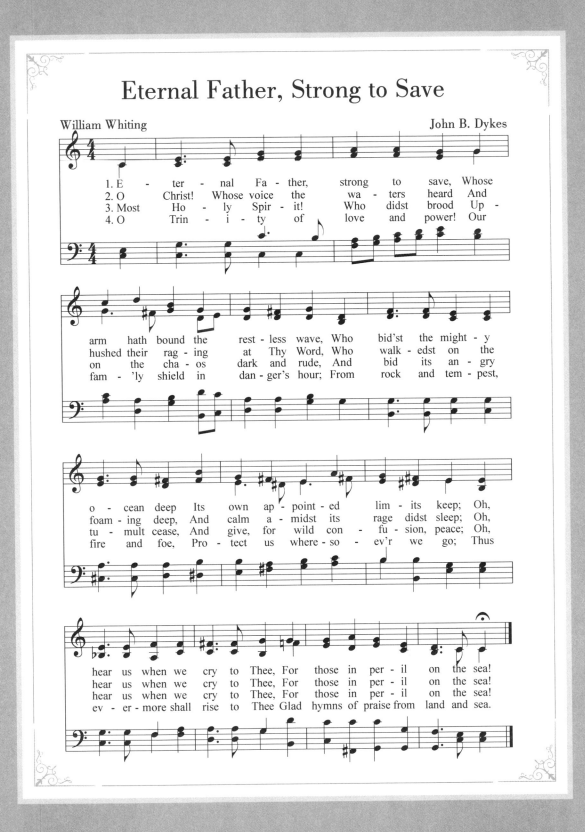

1. E - ter - nal Fa - ther, strong to save, Whose
2. O Christ! Whose voice the wa - ters heard And
3. Most Ho - ly Spir - it! Who didst brood Up -
4. O Trin - i - ty of love and power! Our

arm hath bound the rest - less wave, Who bid'st the might - y
hushed their rag - ing at Thy Word, Who walk - edst on the
on the cha - os dark and rude, And bid its an - gry
fam - 'ly shield in dan - ger's hour; From rock and tem - pest,

o - cean deep Its own ap - point - ed lim - its keep; Oh,
foam - ing deep, And calm a - midst its rage didst sleep; Oh,
tu - mult cease, And give, for wild con - fu - sion, peace; Oh,
fire and foe, Pro - tect us where - so - ev'r we go; Thus

hear us when we cry to Thee, For those in per - il on the sea!
hear us when we cry to Thee, For those in per - il on the sea!
hear us when we cry to Thee, For those in per - il on the sea!
ev - er - more shall rise to Thee Glad hymns of praise from land and sea.

# ETERNAL FATHER, STRONG TO SAVE

1860

P salm 121 has been called the "Traveler's Psalm" because it requests God's watch-care over the comings and goings of His people: "The LORD shall preserve your going out and your coming in from this time forth, and even forevermore."

Nineteenth-century hymnbooks usually had an entire collection of hymns echoing prayers for God's protection of travelers, especially for sailors. *Hymns for Christian Melody*, for example, published in 1832 by Rev. David Marks, contains twenty-four hymns under the section "Mariners." An 1857 hymnal published by the Freewill Baptist Printing Establishment in Dover, New Hampshire, devotes pages 928–943 to hymns for sailors.

The most famous mariners' hymn, "Eternal Father, Strong to Save," was written in 1860. It is called the "Navy Hymn" because of its association with the Naval Academy in Annapolis. It was Franklin Roosevelt's favorite hymn and was sung at his funeral. In November of 1963, its solemn strains accompanied the casket of John F. Kennedy as it was carried up the steps of the U.S. Capitol to lie in state.

The deeply moving melody was written by the famous composer John B. Dykes, who named it MELITA after the island where Paul was shipwrecked in Acts 27.

Little is known about the author of the words, William Whiting of London. He was master of an Anglican school for musicians, and he wrote several hymns; but only "Eternal Father, Strong to Save" is widely sung today. William reportedly wrote this hymn as a prayer for a friend who was preparing to sail to America:

> *Eternal Father, strong to save, / Whose arm hath bound the restless wave, /*
> *Who bid'st the mighty ocean deep / Its own appointed limits keep; /*
> *Oh, hear us when we cry to Thee, / For those in peril on the sea!*

There follows a verse addressed to the Son and one to the Holy Spirit. Then a closing verse requests traveling mercies from the Trinity. In more recent years, other verses have been added by various writers:

- *Lord, guard and guide the men who fly / Through the great spaces in the sky . . .*
- *Eternal Father, Lord of hosts, / Watch over the men who guard our coasts . . .*
- *God, who dost still the restless foam, / Protect the ones we love at home . . .*
- *O Father, King of earth and sea, / We dedicate this ship to Thee . . .*

Behold, He who keeps Israel shall neither slumber nor sleep.

—Psalm 121:4

# REFLECT

· · · · · · · · · · · · · · · · · · · · · · · · · · · · · · · · · · ·

Why do you think this became the most famous "mariners' hymn"?

_____

_____

_____

_____

_____

What is it about traveling that makes us feel especially reliant on God?

_____

_____

_____

_____

_____

What miracle from the Gospels is stanza two referring to?

_____

_____

_____

Psalm 121:4 offers believers what promise?

_____

_____

_____

*Holy Lord, almighty and eternal Father, thank You for Your mercy that has protected me throughout this day. Let me pass through this night peacefully and with a pure mind and body, that rising with purity in the morning, I may serve You gratefully. Amen.*
—ALCUIN OF YORK (c. 735–804)

## PRAYER REQUESTS FOR THE WEEK

_____

_____

# Revive Us Again

William P. Mackay

John J. Husband

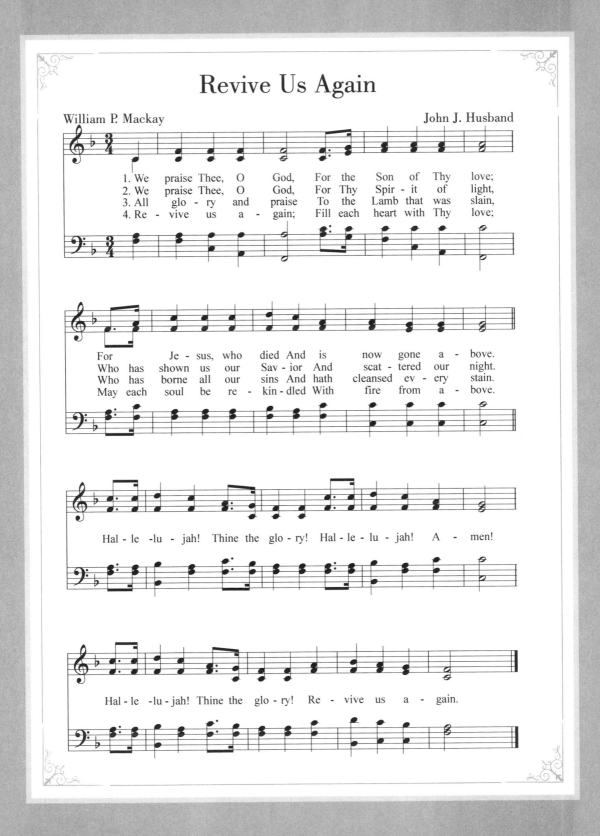

1. We praise Thee, O God, For the Son of Thy love;
2. We praise Thee, O God, For Thy Spir - it of light,
3. All glo - ry and praise To the Lamb that was slain,
4. Re - vive us a - gain; Fill each heart with Thy love;

For Je - sus, who died And is now gone a - bove.
Who has shown us our Sav - ior And scat - tered our night.
Who has borne all our sins And hath cleansed ev - ery stain.
May each soul be re - kin - dled With fire from a - bove.

Hal - le -lu - jah! Thine the glo - ry! Hal - le - lu - jah! A - men!

Hal - le -lu - jah! Thine the glo - ry! Re - vive us a - gain.

# REVIVE US AGAIN

### 1863

In his own words, here is the testimony of Scottish doctor W. P. Mackay, author of "Revive Us Again":

"My dear mother . . . had been a godly, pious woman, quite often telling me of the Savior, and many times I had been a witness to her wrestling in prayer for my soul's salvation. But nothing had made a deep impression on me. The older I grew the more wicked I became. . . .

One day a seriously injured (laborer) . . . was brought into the hospital. The case was hopeless. . . . He seemed to realize his condition, for he was fully conscious, and asked me how long he would last. . . . I gave him my opinion in as cautious a manner as I could. . . .

'Have you any relatives whom we could notify?' I continued.

The patient shook his head. . . . His only wish was to see his landlady, because he owed her a small sum, and also wished to bid her farewell. He also requested his landlady send him, 'The Book. . . .'

I went to see him on my regular visits at least once a day. What struck me most was the quiet, almost happy expression constantly on his face. . . . After the man died, some things about the deceased's affairs were to be attended to in my presence.

'What shall we do with this?' asked the nurse, holding up a book in her hand.

'What kind of book is it?' I asked.

'The Bible of the poor man. . . . As long as he was able to read it, he did so, and when he was unable to do so anymore, he kept it under his bed cover.'

I took the Bible and—could I trust my eyes? It was my own Bible! The Bible which my mother had given me when I left my parents' home, and which later, when short of money, I sold for a small amount. My name was still in it, written in my mother's hand. . . .

With a deep sense of shame I looked upon . . . the precious Book. It had given comfort and refreshing to the unfortunate man in his last hours. It had been a guide to him into eternal life, so that he had been enabled to die in peace and happiness. And this Book, the last gift of my mother, I had actually sold for a ridiculous price. . . .

Be it sufficient to say that the regained possession of my Bible was the cause of my conversion."

Will You not revive us again,
That Your people may rejoice in You?
—PSALM 85:6

# REFLECT

The story of how William P. Mackay found the Bible he'd sold is stranger than fiction, yet it's a true story. Have you ever found something precious that you'd thought was gone forever?

Revisit Philippians 4:6. In light of this, why is it fitting that we sing "Hallelujah! Thine the glory! Hallelujah!" before requesting revival?

See stanza two. How does the Spirit "show us our Savior"?

_____

_____

_____

The text of Psalm 85:6 is very old yet reveals a timeless longing. Recall a time when you experienced a longing for renewal. Did you ask God for help? How was that prayer answered?

_____

_____

_____

> *Lord Jesus, for eternities now, heaven and earth, like fond grandparents, have thrilled at the sight of the children's children ever bringing forth children. . . . And now, amid the starlit night, comes the incomparable Child, the smile of God and tenderness toward mankind. We beg You, Lord, revive in us the joy of Your joy for ever and ever. Amen.*
> —PIERRE TALEC (1933–2016)

## PRAYER REQUESTS FOR THE WEEK

_____

_____

# For the Beauty of the Earth

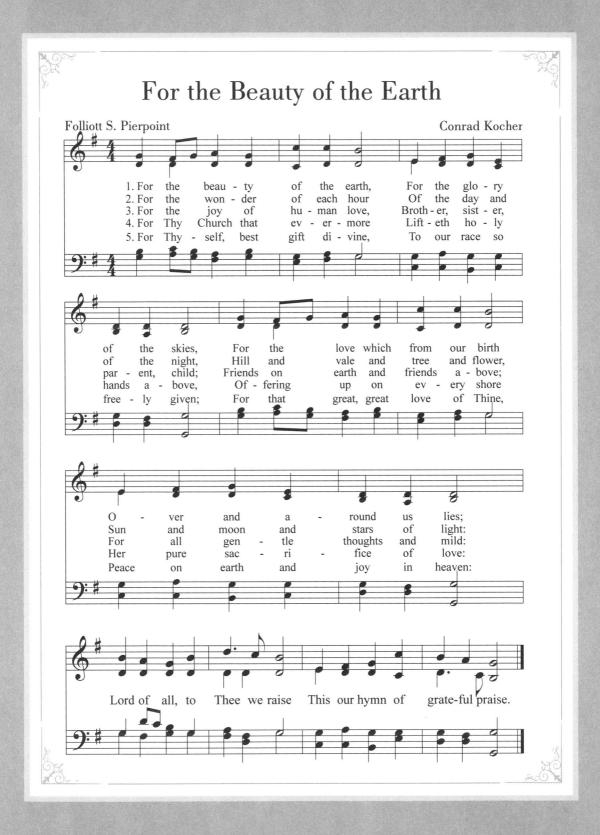

# FOR THE BEAUTY OF THE EARTH

### 1864

Folliott Sandford Pierpoint—that's the unlikely name of the author of this great hymn. Folliott was born October 7, 1835, in Bath, England. After graduating from Cambridge, he taught at Somersetshire College in his home area of Bath.

One day when he was twenty-nine, Folliott found himself walking in the countryside on a beautiful spring day. He saw the ocean of green, the blue dome of heaven, and the winding Avon River cutting through the flowery landscape. Overwhelmed with God's creative brilliance, he wrote this poem. He intended it primarily for Communion services in the Anglican Church, but when it jumped the Atlantic, it quickly became associated with the American Thanksgiving holiday.

In Folliott's original version, each verse ended with "Christ, our God, to Thee we raise / This our sacrifice of praise." That line was eventually changed to, "Lord of all, to Thee we raise / This our hymn of grateful praise."

Little else is known about Folliott Sandford Pierpoint. He resigned from his position at Somersetshire and apparently moved from place to place, teaching some, writing hymns, and publishing his poetry. He died in 1917.

"For the Beauty of the Earth" is one of only a few songs devoted purely to giving thanks. One of the strange things about the "attitude of gratitude" is that we tend to exhibit it in reverse proportion to the number of blessings received. The more we have, the less thankful we are.

Among the lessons Viktor Frankl learned in the Nazi death-camp Auschwitz was to take time to be thankful and to count your blessings. He wrote that prisoners in the camp dreamed at night about certain things more than others. Bread, cakes, and nice warm baths—the very things we take for granted every day.

Ralph Waldo Emerson observed that if the constellations appeared only once in a thousand years, imagine what an exciting event it would be. But because they're there every night, we barely give them a look.

One of the evidences of the Holy Spirit's work in our lives is a gradual reversal of that twisted pattern. God wants to make us people who exhibit a thankfulness in proper proportion to the gifts and blessings we've received.

Why not take time to sing this hymn to the Lord right now?

Therefore You are great, O Lord God. For there is none like You, nor is there any God besides You, according to all that we have heard with our ears.

—2 Samuel 7:22

# REFLECT

· · · · · · · · · · · · · · · · · · · · · · · · · · · · · · · · · ·

This passage points out a bizarre phenomenon—that we often "exhibit [gratitude] in reverse proportion to the number of blessings received." Why do you suppose this is?

Consider Ralph Waldo Emerson's observation about the constellations. Try offering up a prayer right now in gratitude for something you've experienced often in nature.

_____

_____

_____

_____

Why would the author originally have thought this hymn appropriate for Communion services?

_____

_____

_____

Consider the original line "Christ, our God, to Thee we raise / This our sacrifice of praise" versus the eventual "Lord of all, to Thee we raise / This our hymn of grateful praise." Which do you prefer and why?

_____

_____

_____

> _O God, who hast made the most sacred night to shine with illumination of the true light, grant, we beseech Thee, that, as we have known the mystery of that light upon earth, we may also perfectly enjoy it in heaven; through the same Jesus Christ our Lord. Amen._
> —GELASIAN SACRAMENTARY (8TH C.)

## PRAYER REQUESTS FOR THE WEEK

_____

_____

# My Jesus, I Love Thee

# MY JESUS, I LOVE THEE

### 1864

The young people of today are utterly dissolute and disorderly," fumed grumpy old Martin Luther in the sixteenth century. The philosopher Plato agreed. "The youth are rebellious, pleasure-seeking, and irresponsible," he wrote. "They have no respect for their elders." Socrates complained, "Children now love luxury. They have bad manners, contempt for authority. They show disrespect for elders, and love chatter."

A six-thousand-year-old Egyptian tomb bears this inscription: "We live in a decadent age. Young people no longer respect their parents. They are rude and impatient. They inhabit taverns and have no self-control."

The next time you think the "modern generation" is going from bad to worse, remember that God always has a rich handful of teenage heroes ready to change the world. In Bible times, we read of Joseph the dreamer, Daniel in Babylon, David the giant-killer, and the virgin Mary (likely still a teen).

As a teenager, Charles Spurgeon preached to great crowds, but when they referred to his youthfulness, he replied, "Never mind my age. Think of the Lord Jesus Christ and His preciousness."

In our own day, we've been deeply moved by young people like seventeen-year-old Cassie Bernall of Littleton, Colorado, who was shot for her faith during the Columbine tragedy.

Some of our greatest hymns were also written by young adults. Isaac Watts wrote most of his most memorable hymns at about the age of nineteen. When poet John Milton was fifteen, he wrote the well-known "Let Us with a Gladsome Mind." The hymn "Work, for the Night Is Coming" was written by an eighteen-year-old. And this hymn of deep devotion, "My Jesus, I Love Thee," was written by William Ralph Featherston at age sixteen. Sixteen!

Featherston was born July 23, 1846, in Montreal. He died in the same city twenty-six years later. His family attended the Wesleyan Methodist Church, and it seems likely that William wrote this hymn as a poem celebrating his conversion to Christ. Reportedly, he sent it to an aunt living in California, and somehow it was published as an anonymous hymn in a British hymnal in 1864.

Little else is known about the origin of the hymn or its author, but that's all right. It's enough just to know that God can change the world through anyone—regardless of age—who will say, "My Jesus, I love Thee; I know Thou art mine. For Thee all the follies of sin I resign."

We love Him because He first loved us.
—1 John 4:19

# REFLECT

Adults sometimes dismiss or discredit young people based on their chronological age. Have you been guilty of this? Were you dismissed as a young person too? What does 1 Timothy 4:12 say about youth?

_____

_____

_____

_____

Do you see anything in William R. Featherston's lyrics that reveals the hymn was written by a young person?

_____

_____

_____

_____

Notice the repetition of "brow" in the last three verses—first regarding Christ's brow and then twice referring to the author's own brow. Contrast the three uses.

_____

_____

_____

Consider the lines "For Thee all the follies / Of sin I resign." What does resigning from these follies require?

_____

_____

_____

_Look down upon me, good and gentle Jesus, while before Your face I humbly kneel and with burning soul pray and beseech You to fix deep in my heart lively sentiments of faith, hope, and charity, true contrition for my sins, and a firm purpose of amendment. I contemplate, with great love, and tender pity, Your five most precious wounds, pondering over them within me and calling to mind the words that David, Your prophet, said of You, my Jesus: "They have pierced My hands and My feet, they have numbered My bones." Amen._
—TRADITIONAL CATHOLIC PRAYER

## PRAYER REQUESTS FOR THE WEEK

_____

_____

# SPIRIT OF GOD, DESCEND UPON MY HEART

## 1854

This hymn, so often sung on Pentecost Sunday, is a deeply moving prayer for personal devotion or church use anytime. Its author, George Croly, was born in Dublin in 1780. His father was a physician, but George decided to become a physician of souls and was ordained into the Anglican ministry when he graduated from Trinity College in Dublin in 1804. No church became available to him, so he moved to London, started writing, and developed a respected reputation as a gifted man of letters.

Eventually Croly was assigned to St. Stephen's, a church in the slums of London that had been closed for a hundred years. There Croly preached eloquent sermons without notes, and the crowds came. He spoke extemporaneously, sometimes changing his mind mid-service about his subject or text. His energy was boundless as he churned out seemingly endless compositions—hymns, dramas, biographies, historical and theological works, sermons, and novels.

In 1854, Croly published a volume of hymns entitled *Psalms and Hymns for Public Worship*. Just before the book was released, fire broke out and destroyed most of the copies. Extant copies are now extremely rare. But one hymn from the book has lived on—Croly's prayer to the Holy Spirit: "Spirit of God, Descend upon My Heart." He based it on Galatians 5:25—"If we live in the Spirit, let us also walk in the Spirit" (KJV).

Dr. Croly was described as tall, with a massive chest and head, short stubby iron-gray hair, a broad furrowed forehead, large gray eyes, a wide mouth, and an ample chin. He enjoyed good health until old age, but following the Christmas Day death of his son in a war in India and the subsequent passing of his wife, his strength declined. On November 24, 1860, leaving his home in Bloomsbury Square for a regular Saturday afternoon walk, he collapsed and was carried into a nearby shop where he was pronounced dead in his eightieth year.

## VERSE OF THE WEEK

When the day of Pentecost came, they were all together in one place. Suddenly a sound like the blowing of a violent wind came from heaven and filled the whole house where they were sitting. They saw what seemed to be tongues of fire that separated and came to rest on each of them.

—Acts 2:1–3 (NIV)

# REFLECT

We read about how a fire destroyed almost all the copies of the author's volume of hymns. Have you ever lost something in which you'd invested a great deal of time and energy? How did you recover?

_____

_____

_____

How might God "wean" our hearts from earth?

_____

_____

_____

What does the author mean by "dimness" of the soul? Can you empathize with this?

_____

_____

_____

How do we "walk in the Spirit" (Galatians 5:25)?

_____

_____

_____

*Spirit of God, with Your holy breath You cleanse the hearts and minds of Your people; You comfort them when they are in sorrow; You lead them when they wander from the way; You kindle them when they are cold; You knot them together when they are at variance; and You enrich them with many and various gifts. We beseech You daily to increase those gifts which You have entrusted to us; that with Your light before us and within us we may pass through this world without stumbling and without straying. Amen.*

—ERASMUS (1466–1536)

## PRAYER REQUESTS FOR THE WEEK

_____

_____

# O Love That Wilt Not Let Me Go

George Matheson

Albert L. Peace

1. O love that wilt not let me go, I
2. O light that fol-low'st all my way, I
3. O joy that seek-est me through pain, I
4. O cross that lift-est up my head, I

rest my wea-ry soul in Thee. I give Thee back the
yield my flick-'ring torch to Thee. My heart re-stores its
can-not close my heart to Thee. I trace the rain-bow
dare not ask to fly from Thee. I lay in dust life's

life I owe, That in Thine o-cean depths its
bor-rowed ray, That in Thy sun-shine's blaze its
through the rain, And feel the prom-ise is not
glo-ry dead, And from the ground there blos-soms

flow, May rich-er, full - - er be.
day, May bright-er, fair - - er be.
vain, That morn shall tear - - less be.
red, Life that shall end - - less be.

# O LOVE THAT WILT NOT LET ME GO

### 1882

George Matheson was only a teenager when he learned that his poor eyesight was deteriorating further. Not to be denied, he continued straightaway with his plans to enroll in Glasgow University, and his determination led to his graduating at age nineteen. But as he pursued graduate studies for Christian ministry, he became totally blind. His sisters joined ranks beside him, learning Greek and Hebrew to assist him in his studies, and he pressed faithfully on. But his spirit collapsed when his fiancée, unwilling to be married to a blind man, broke their engagement and returned his ring.

George never married, and the pain of that rejection never totally left him. Years later, his sister came to him, announcing her engagement. He rejoiced with her, but his mind went back to his own heartache. He consoled himself by thinking of God's love, which is never limited, never conditional, never withdrawn, and never uncertain. Out of this experience it is said he wrote the hymn "O Love That Wilt Not Let Me Go" on June 6, 1882.

．．．．．．．．．．

George Matheson became a powerful and popular preacher pastoring in the Scottish village of Innellan. Despite his flourishing ministry, there was one winter's evening when the Sunday night crowd was miserably small. George had worked hard on his sermon, but the empty chairs nearly defeated him. Nevertheless he did his best, not knowing that in the congregation was a visitor from the large St. Bernard's Church in Edinburgh, which was seeking a pastor. As a result, in 1886, he was called to St. Bernard's where he became one of Scotland's favorite preachers.

"Make every occasion a great occasion," Matheson later said. "You can never tell when somebody may be taking your measure for a larger place."

．．．．．．．．．．

Recently while in Edinburgh, I tracked down George Matheson's old church, St. Bernard's, in a lovely residential neighborhood not far from Princes Street. The doors were locked shut, and this curious notice was posted to the front door:

PUBLIC ENTERTAINMENT LICENSE
THE PREMISES WILL BE USED AS A CONCERT AND DANCE HALL,
AND FOR NO OTHER PURPOSE WITHOUT WRITTEN
PERMISSION FROM THE COUNCIL.

# REFLECT

Author George Matheson purportedly wrote this hymn in response to his own heartache at having been rejected by his fiancée. For you, which line from the hymn feels most in contrast to romantic love?

_____

_____

_____

_____

Consider the story in this passage about Matheson preaching to a tiny crowd on a Sunday night. How might his life have turned out differently had he let discouragement overtake him? Do his words about making "every occasion a great occasion" ring true for you?

_____

_____

_____

_____

Verse one says, "I rest my weary soul in Thee." What does Isaiah 30:15 say about rest?

_____

_____

_____

See verse three. What divine attribute does the hymn say "seeks" us through pain? Have you experienced this? When and how?

_____

_____

_____

*Come, O Love, O God, Thou alone art all my love in verity. Thou art my dearest Salvation, all my hope and my joy, my supreme and surpassing Good. In the morning I will stand before Thee, my God, and will contemplate Thee, my dearest Love, because Thou art pure delightsomeness and sweetness eternal. Thou art the thirst of my heart; Thou art all the sufficiency of my spirit. The more I taste Thee, the more I hunger; the more I drink, the more I thirst. Amen.*
—GERTRUDE THE GREAT (1256–C. 1302)

## PRAYER REQUESTS FOR THE WEEK

_____

_____

# Near to the Heart of God

Cleland B. McAfee

Cleland B. McAfee

1. There is a place of qui - et rest, Near to the heart of God;
2. There is a place of com - fort sweet, Near to the heart of God;
3. There is a place of full re - lease, Near to the heart of God;

A place where sin can - not mo - lest, Near to the heart of God.
A place where we our Sav - ior meet, Near to the heart of God.
A place where all is joy and peace, Near to the heart of God.

O Je - sus, blest Re - deem - er, Sent from the heart of God,

Hold us, who wait be - fore Thee, Near to the heart of God.

# NEAR TO THE HEART OF GOD

1903

Park University in Parkville, Missouri, with thirty-eight campuses across the United States, boasts of an enrollment of twenty-three thousand students. It was begun in 1875, with only seventeen students, by John A. McAfee and Colonel George Park, the colorful founder of Parkville, who donated the land.

McAfee had five sons and a daughter who all became involved in the college. The fourth son, Cleland, graduated from what was then Park College; after studying at Union Theological Seminary, he returned to Park as chaplain and choir director. Cleland's daughter, Katharine, later told how her father came to write the great hymn "Near to the Heart of God":

> My father's father, John A. McAfee, was one of the founders and the first president of Park College in Missouri. In the last years of the past century, his five sons (Lowell, Howard, Lapsley, Cleland, Ernest) and his only daughter (Helen) were all living in Parkville, serving the college. My father was the college preacher and director of the choir, and it was his custom, when Communion services came, to write the words and music of a response which his choir could sing and which would fit into the theme of his sermon.
>
> One terrible week, just before a Communion Sunday, the two little daughters of my Uncle Howard and Aunt Lucy McAfee died of diphtheria within twenty-four hours of each other. The college family and town were stricken with grief. My father often told us how he sat long and late thinking of what could be said in word and song on the coming Sunday. . . .
>
> So he wrote ["Near to the Heart of God"]. The choir learned it at the regular Saturday night rehearsal, and afterward they went to Howard McAfee's home and sang it as they stood under the sky outside the darkened, quarantined house. It was sung again on Sunday morning at the Communion service.

"Near to the Heart of God" was published in October 1903 in *The Choir Leader*. In later years, Cleland pastored in the Presbyterian denomination, taught at McCormick Theological Seminary in Chicago, and helped direct the Presbyterian foreign missions program. He is the author of a number of textbooks, including *The Greatest English Classic: A Study of the King James Version and Its Influence,* and *Ministerial Practices: Some Fraternal Suggestions,* published in 1928.

He will gather the lambs with His arm, and carry them in His bosom.

—Isaiah 40:11

# REFLECT

· · · · · · · · · · · · · · · · · · · · · · · · · · · · · · ·

This passage shares that the author wrote this hymn for the Communion service after the deaths of his two little nieces. How might this song be especially poignant in light of the passing of a loved one?

_____

_____

_____

_____

Do you think the "place" described in the song is a physical place? Why or why not?

_____

_____

_____

_____

What image does Isaiah 40:11 use to portray the heart of God toward us?

_____

_____

_____

According to the chorus, who holds us "near to the heart of God"?

_____

_____

_____

> _Let the eternal God be the portion of my soul; let heaven be my inheritance and hope; let Christ be my Head, and my promise of security; let faith be my wisdom, and love my very heart and will, and patient persevering obedience be my life; and then I can spare the wisdom of the world, because I can spare the trifles that it seeks, and all that they are like to get by it. Amen._
>
> —RICHARD BAXTER (1615–1691)

## PRAYER REQUESTS FOR THE WEEK

_____

_____

# Precious Lord, Take My Hand

Thomas A. Dorsey

George N. Allen

1. Pre - cious Lord, take my hand, Lead me on, help me
2. When my way grows drear, Pre - cious Lord, lin - ger

stand; I am tired, I am weak, I am worn;
near; When my life is al - most gone,

Thru the storm, thru the night, Lead me on to the
Hear my cry, hear my call, Hold my hand lest I

light, Take my hand, precious Lord, lead me home.
fall; Take my hand, pre-cious Lord, lead me home.

# PRECIOUS LORD, TAKE MY HAND

1932

Some people think this great old gospel song was written by the famous big band leader Tommy Dorsey. It wasn't; the author was named Thomas Andrew Dorsey, and he was the son of a black revivalist preacher.

Thomas was born in a small town in Georgia in 1899. When he was about eleven, the Dorseys moved to Atlanta where Thomas was quickly enamored with the blues and began playing piano at a vaudeville theater. Later the family moved to Chicago where he attended classes at the College of Composition and Arranging. Soon he was onstage under the name "Georgia Tom," playing barrelhouse piano in one of Al Capone's Chicago speakeasies and leading jazz bands.

Thomas was converted at the National Baptist Convention in Chicago in 1921, and began writing gospel songs and trying to get them published. It was discouraging at first. He later said, "I borrowed five dollars and sent out five hundred copies of my song, 'If You See My Savior,' to churches throughout the country. . . . It was three years before I got a single order. I felt like going back to the blues."

He didn't, and gradually his reputation grew and his work became known.

In August 1932, while leading music in St. Louis, he was handed a telegram bearing the words, "Your wife just died." He rushed to a phone to call home, but all he could hear over the line was "Nettie is dead! Nettie is dead!" A friend drove him through the night, and he arrived home to learn that his baby boy had also died.

"I began to feel that God had done me an injustice," Thomas later said. "I didn't want to serve Him anymore or write any more gospel songs." But the next Saturday, while alone in a friend's music room, he had a "strange feeling" inside—a sudden calm and a quiet stillness. "As my fingers began to manipulate over the keys, words began to fall in place on the melody like drops of water falling from the crevice of the rock":

*Precious Lord, take my hand,*
*Lead me on, help me stand;*
*I am tired, I am weak, I am worn.*

Today Thomas A. Dorsey is remembered as the "Father of Gospel Music" and the author of hundreds of gospel songs including his equally famous hymn "Peace in the Valley."

Be strong and of good courage, do not fear nor be afraid of them; for the LORD your God, He is the One who goes with you. He will not leave you nor forsake you.

—DEUTERONOMY 31:6

# REFLECT

Thomas A. Dorsey, now known as the "Father of Gospel Music," began his career as a blues man. Do you see anything in this hymn that reflects these origins?

_____

_____

_____

_____

Dorsey reports that the words and melody seemed to flow "like drops of water falling from the crevice of the rock." Does this image hold any biblical significance?

_____

_____

_____

_____

The imagery of the song portrays being led by the hand. What is the destination of that leading?

_____

_____

_____

Does the promise of Deuteronomy 31:6 mean something special to you today?

_____

_____

_____

*As the hand is made for holding and the eye for seeing, You have created me for joy, O God. Share with me in finding that joy everywhere: in the violet's beauty, in the lark's melody, in the child's face, in a mother's love, in the purity of Jesus. Amen.*
—TRADITIONAL SCOTTISH GAELIC PRAYER

## PRAYER REQUESTS FOR THE WEEK

_____

_____

# We Gather Together

Anonymous Dutch Hymn

Dutch Folk Song

1. We gath - er to - geth - er to ask the Lord's bless-ing;
2. Be - side us to guide us, our God with us join-ing,
3. We all do ex - tol Thee, Thou Lead - er tri - um-phant,

He chas - tens and has - tens His will to make known;
Or - dain-ing, main-tain - ing His king - dom di - vine;
And pray that Thou still our De - fend - er wilt be.

The wick - ed op - press-ing now cease from dis-tress-ing,
So from the be - gin - ning the fight we were win-ning:
Let Thy con - gre - ga - tion es - cape tri - bu - la - tion:

Sing prais - es to His name: He for - gets not His own.
Thou, Lord, wast at our side, all glo - ry be Thine!
Thy Name be ev - er praised! O Lord, make us free!

# WE GATHER TOGETHER

1597

Those who have visited the Netherlands with its picturesque dikes and windmills may be unaware of the terrific struggle for religious freedom that took place there in the sixteenth and seventeenth centuries. In 1555, the Low Country was given to King Philip II of Spain by his father, Emperor Charles V of Germany. Philip was an arch-Catholic, but the winds of Calvinistic Reformation had reached the Netherlands. Roman Catholic churches were plundered, and the authority of Spain was resisted.

In 1557, King Philip sent the dreaded Duke of Alba (Fernando Alvarez de Toledo) to bring the Netherlands back into the Pope's fold. He established a reign of terror during which ten thousand people were executed and another forty thousand exiled. His ruling council was called the "Council of Troubles," but it's better known to history as the "Blood Council." The bodies of thousands of people were hung in the streets and on the doorposts of houses. Alva didn't hesitate to massacre whole cities. An attack on Leiden was stopped only by cutting the dikes and flooding the countryside.

On January 6, 1579, the Catholic southern regions of the Netherlands (modern Belgium) declared their allegiance to Philip; but three weeks later the northern part (modern Holland) refused to submit to the Catholic rule of Spain. In 1581, Holland declared its independence, led by the courageous William of Orange. Holland was devastated by warfare, and in the process William was cut down by an assassin's dagger. But the brave nation would not be denied, and eventually Spain lost its hold on the Dutch Republic.

This hymn, "We Gather Together," which Americans associate with their Thanksgiving holiday, was actually written sometime in 1597 to celebrate Holland's freedom from Spain. Its author, an unknown Dutchman, was full of thanksgiving that his people were finally free from Spanish tyranny and free to worship as they chose. Notice how he expressed this theme in these three beautiful verses:

*The wicked oppressing now cease from distressing . . .*
*So from the beginning the fight we were winning:*
*Thou, Lord, wast at our side, all glory be Thine!*
*We all do extol Thee, Thou Leader triumphant,*
*And pray that Thou still our Defender wilt be.*
*Let Thy congregation escape tribulation:*
*Thy Name be ever praised! O Lord, make us free!*

115

So the nations shall fear the name of the LORD,
And all the kings of the earth Your glory.

—PSALM 102:15

# REFLECT

This hymn was written to celebrate Holland's freedom. How do the lyrics reflect the terrible suffering the Dutch had endured?

_____

_____

_____

_____

_____

The historical context is helpful in understanding why these lyrics often refer to battle. How do you relate to warfare?

_____

_____

_____

_____

_____

How do you feel when you "gather together" with other believers?

_____

_____

_____

The hymn states that God "forgets not His own." How does this line up with the promise of Deuteronomy 31:6?

_____

_____

_____

*Heavenly Father, receive my evening sacrifice of praise, and confession, and prayer, I beseech Thee. I thank Thee for all the known and unknown mercies of another day, for all the blessings of this life, for all the means of grace, for all the riches of Thy salvation, and for the hope of glory, that blessed hope, the coming of our Lord Jesus Christ and our gathering together unto Him. We are one day nearer to that day. Teach us to live every day as those whose citizenship is in heaven. Amen.*
—HANDLEY CARR GLYN MOULE (1841–1920)

## PRAYER REQUESTS FOR THE WEEK

_____

_____

# Love Divine, All Loves Excelling

Charles Wesley

John Zundel

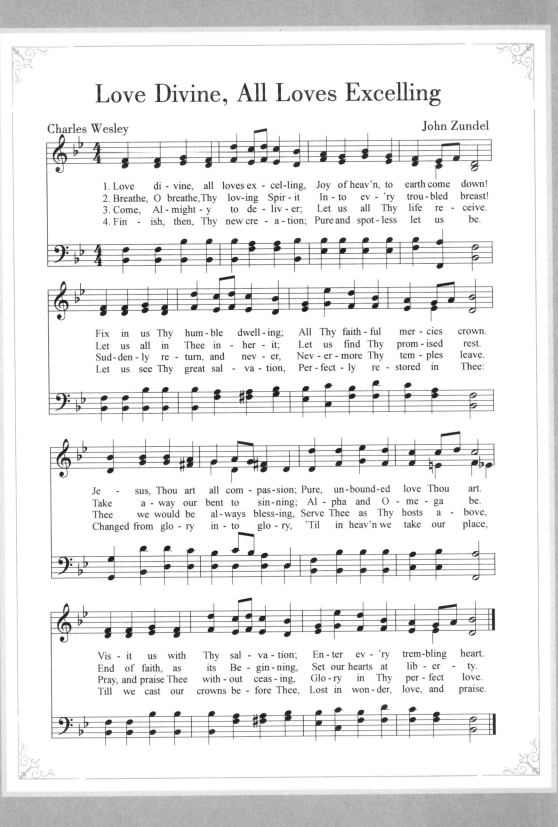

1. Love di - vine, all loves ex - cel - ling, Joy of heav'n, to earth come down!
2. Breathe, O breathe, Thy lov - ing Spir - it In - to ev - 'ry trou - bled breast!
3. Come, Al - might - y to de - liv - er; Let us all Thy life re - ceive.
4. Fin - ish, then, Thy new cre - a - tion; Pure and spot - less let us be.

Fix in us Thy hum - ble dwell - ing; All Thy faith - ful mer - cies crown.
Let us all in Thee in - her - it; Let us find Thy prom - ised rest.
Sud - den - ly re - turn, and nev - er, Nev - er - more Thy tem - ples leave.
Let us see Thy great sal - va - tion, Per - fect - ly re - stored in Thee:

Je - sus, Thou art all com - pas - sion; Pure, un - bound - ed love Thou art.
Take a - way our bent to sin - ning; Al - pha and O - me - ga be.
Thee we would be al - ways bless - ing, Serve Thee as Thy hosts a - bove,
Changed from glo - ry in - to glo - ry, 'Til in heav'n we take our place,

Vis - it us with Thy sal - va - tion; En - ter ev - 'ry trem - bling heart.
End of faith, as its Be - gin - ning, Set our hearts at lib - er - ty.
Pray, and praise Thee with - out ceas - ing, Glo - ry in Thy per - fect love.
Till we cast our crowns be - fore Thee, Lost in won - der, love, and praise.

# LOVE DIVINE, ALL LOVES EXCELLING

1747

After their marriage, Charles and Sally Wesley set up housekeeping in Bristol, England, heading up the Methodist activities there. Later they moved to London so Charles could work more closely with his brother, John. All the while, however, he was writing hymns. There are few stories behind specific hymns because Charles was just always writing them. He didn't need events to inspire him or quiet stretches of meditative time in which to develop his thoughts. He was just always writing hymns, and afterward he had few if any dramatic stories to tell about the occasions for writing them.

Biographer Arnold Dallimore says about his poetry: "He had inherited this gift from his father and although it had undoubtedly been resident in him since childhood, his conversion unlocked it and set it free. During [his] early ministry he says little in his journal about his composing hymns and, indeed, this is true throughout his life. But he had within him virtually a treasury of poetry. He constantly experienced the emotions of the true poet, his mind instinctively invested words with harmony, and hymn after hymn flowed from his pen."

Henry Moore, one of his friends, later described Charles like this: "When he was nearly eighty he rode a little horse, gray with age. . . . Even in the height of summer he was dressed in winter clothes. As he jogged leisurely along, he jotted down any thought that struck him. He kept a card in his pocket for this purpose, on which he wrote his hymn in shorthand. Not infrequently he had come to our house in City Road, and, having left the pony in the garden in front, he would enter, crying out, 'Pen and ink! Pen and ink!' These being supplied he wrote the hymn he had been composing."

How many hymns did Wesley compose? No one has been able to count them. In all, Charles wrote over nine thousand literary texts of one kind or another, but not all of them should be classified as hymns. Experts put the number somewhere between three thousand and six thousand. Among all of them, "Love Divine, All Loves Excelling" is the favorite of many.

Charles's last hymn was dictated to his beloved Sally as he was on his deathbed in March 1788. It was short, simple, and picturesque. Predictably, it, too, became a popular one-verse song among the Methodists:

> *In age and feebleness extreme, / Who shall a helpless worm redeem?*
> *Jesus, my only hope Thou art, / Strength of my failing flesh and heart,*
> *Oh, could I catch a smile from Thee / And drop into eternity!*

## VERSE OF THE WEEK

His divine power has given to us all things that pertain to life and godliness, through the knowledge of Him who called us by glory and virtue.

—2 PETER 1:3

## REFLECT

· · · · · · · · · · · · · · · · · · · · · · · · · · · · · · · · · · · · · ·

The passage notes that the prolific Charles Wesley kept a card in his pocket to jot down lyrics. How do you keep track of thoughts that encourage or inspire you?

_____

_____

_____

_____

Whom, specifically, does the author call "Love divine"?

_____

_____

_____

_____

The language of this hymn is beautiful but perhaps can obscure meaning. How does Jesus' love "excel" other loves?

_____

_____

_____

Verse three says, "Nevermore Thy temples leave." How does this pertain to the promise of 1 Corinthians 6:19?

_____

_____

_____

> _Lo, fainter now lie spread the shades of night, and upward spread the trembling gleams of morn; suppliant we bend before the Lord of Light, and pray at early dawn that His sweet charity may all our sin forgive, and make our miseries to cease; may grant us health, grant us the gift divine of everlasting peace. Father Supreme, this grace on us confer, and Thou, O Son, by an eternal birth, with Thee, coequal Spirit comforter, whose glory fills the earth! Amen._
>
> —GREGORY THE GREAT (540–604)

## PRAYER REQUESTS FOR THE WEEK

_____

_____

# Savior, Like a Shepherd Lead Us

# SAVIOR, LIKE A SHEPHERD LEAD US

### 1836

This hymn, originally for children, first appeared in an 1836 volume entitled *Hymns for the Young*, compiled by Dorothy A. Thrupp. Many hymnologists have attributed the words to Mrs. Thrupp, but her authorship is uncertain. One early hymnbook attributed it to Henry Francis Lyte; but that, too, is doubtful.

There's no doubt, however, about the composer of the music. It was the famous William Bradbury, one of the most prolific hymnists of the nineteenth century. A native of York, Maine, William moved to Boston at age fourteen to enroll in the Boston Academy of Music. There he joined Lowell Mason's choir at the Bowdoin Street Church.

Lowell Mason was a banker-turned-composer who became the first American to receive a doctorate in music from an American university. A dedicated Christian, he had written the tunes for such hymns as "Joy to the World!," "My Faith Looks Up to Thee," "Nearer, My God, to Thee," and "From Greenland's Icy Mountains." Mason was passionate about training children in sacred music.

Recognizing that young William Bradbury had an inborn talent, Mason sought to encourage him at every turn. Soon William was playing the organ under Mason's watchful eye, and earning a whopping $25 a year in the process.

William was so inspired by his mentor that he moved to New York City to do there what Mason had been doing in Boston—encouraging the Christian musical education of children. He organized and led children's singing conventions, encouraged music in the New York school system, and published Sunday school songbooks. During his lifetime, fifty-nine separate books appeared under his name.

Bradbury set in motion a great change in American church music. Prior to his work, most hymns were heavy, noble, and stately. William wanted to write lighter melodies that children could sing. His compositions were softer, full of movement, and easier for children to sing.

In so doing, William Bradbury helped usher in the era of gospel music. He may not have realized that adults would sing his hymns as readily as children would, but he paved the way for the likes of Fanny Crosby and Ira Sankey. Today Bradbury is remembered as the musical composer of such favorites as "He Leadeth Me," "The Solid Rock," "Just As I Am," "Jesus Loves Me," "Sweet Hour of Prayer," and this one—"Savior, Like a Shepherd Lead Us."

For the Lamb who is in the midst of the throne will shepherd them and lead them to living fountains of waters. And God will wipe away every tear from their eyes.

—REVELATION 7:17

## REFLECT

The passage tells us that the author's intention was to write lighter melodies specifically for children to sing. What about this hymn feels soft or light to you? How does it lift your spirits?

_____

_____

_____

_____

This song calls Jesus a Shepherd and specifically in verse one refers to "pleasant pastures." Which of the psalms does this call to mind for you?

_____

_____

_____

_____

Verse three confesses our sinful condition. What does it mean to "early turn to Thee"?

_____

_____

_____

What is the promise of Revelation 7:17?

_____

_____

_____

> *O good Shepherd, seek me, and bring me home to Your fold again. . . . Deal favorably with me according to Your grace, till I may dwell in Your house all the days of my life, and praise You for ever and ever with those who are there. Amen.*
>
> —JEROME (347–420)

## PRAYER REQUESTS FOR THE WEEK

_____

_____

# Jesus, Savior, Pilot Me

# JESUS, SAVIOR, PILOT ME

1871

Visitors to Manhattan should take time to visit the First Chinese Presbyterian Church at the corner of Henry Street and Market on the Lower East Side, not far from the Manhattan and Brooklyn Bridges. This grand old building is a Gothic historical landmark, the second oldest church building in New York City. Dutch Reformed Christians built it in 1819. When that group disbanded their church in 1864, the building was acquired by another congregation who chose an unusual name for their church: the Church of Sea and Land.

This was the busy harbor section of New York, with thousands of sailors filling the streets every day. The pastor of the Church of Sea and Land was Edward Hopper, a lifelong New Yorker and a graduate of both the University of the City of New York and Union Theological Seminary in the heart of Manhattan. After pastorates in Greenville, New York, and later in Long Island, Hopper returned to Manhattan to engage in pastoral and evangelistic work among the sailors. Hopper often composed hymns for his sailors, including one titled "Wrecked and Struggling in Mid-Ocean."

On May 3, 1871, this poem-prayer, "Jesus, Savior, Pilot Me," appeared without attribution in *The Sailor's Magazine.*

In Philadelphia, an ailing composer named John Edgar Gould saw a copy of this poem and, deeply moved, composed music for it the night before he sailed to Africa in an effort to regain his health. Gould died in Algiers four years later. But "Jesus, Savior, Pilot Me" developed a healthy following in churches across America, especially among those ministering to seafaring men. The sailors and parishioners at the Church of Sea and Land numbered this among their favorite hymns, dubbing it "The Sailor's Hymn," though they had no idea that their own pastor was its author. That fact remained hidden for years, until Hopper finally disclosed it at a special anniversary celebration of New York's Seamen's Friend Society.

On April 23, 1888, suffering from heart disease, Hopper sat in the easy chair of his study, preparing to write another hymn. At the top of the page he put its title—"Heaven"—then he slumped over dead. Among the papers found in his study was the original manuscript of "Jesus, Savior, Pilot Me."

"Why are you fearful, O you of little faith?" Then He arose and rebuked the winds and the sea, and there was a great calm.

—MATTHEW 8:26

# REFLECT

The author of this song had a special ministry to sailors. How might sailors' needs have differed from those of ordinary parishioners of the time?

Though John E. Gould composed the music to accompany Hopper's lyrics, the two never met. Have you ever collaborated with a stranger or built upon something a stranger started?

What does the phrase "pilot me" mean in this hymn? What is your heart's prayer?

_____

_____

This song makes reference to Matthew chapter 8, where we read that Jesus calmed the winds and sea when his disciples were feeling panicked. What are you feeling nervous about right now? Ask Jesus to speak peace into that area of your life right now.

_____

_____

_____

> *Ah, Lord, to whom all hearts are open, You can pilot the ship of my soul far better than I can. . . . Do not let me be carried hither and thither by wandering thoughts, but, forgetting all else, let me see and hear You alone. Renew my spirit; kindle in me Your light, that it may shine within me, and my heart may burn in love and adoration for You. Let Your Holy Spirit dwell in me continually, and make me Your temple and sanctuary. Fill me with divine love and light and life, with devout and heavenly thoughts, with comfort and strength, with joy and peace. Amen.*
> —JOHANN ARNDT (1555–1621)

## PRAYER REQUESTS FOR THE WEEK

_____

_____

# Whiter Than Snow

James Nicholson

William G. Fischer

1. Lord Je - sus, I long to be per - fect - ly whole; I
2. Lord Je - sus, look down from Thy throne in the skies And
3. Lord Je - sus, be - fore You I pa - tient - ly wait; Come

want Thee for - ev - er to live in my soul. Break down ev - ery
help me to make a com - plete sac - ri - fice. I give up my-
now and with - in me a new heart cre - ate. To those who have

i - dol, cast out ev - ery foe. Now wash me and I shall be
self and what - ev - er I know, Now wash me and I shall be
sought Thee, Thou nev - er saidst, "No." Now wash me and I shall be

whit - er than snow. Whit - er than snow, Yes, whit - er than

snow, Now wash me and I shall be Whit - er than snow.

# WHITER THAN SNOW

1872

James Nicholson, author of "Whiter Than Snow," was a dedicated Christian who lived in Washington, D.C., where he worked for the post office. Born in Ireland in the 1820s, James had immigrated to America in the 1850s, originally settling in Philadelphia where he became active in the Wharton Street Methodist Episcopal Church as a Sunday school and evangelistic worker. In 1871, he moved to Washington to assume his new duties with the post office, and the next year he published this hymn.

"Whiter Than Snow" is based on Psalm 51:7, the prayer of repentance offered by King David after his sin with Bathsheba: "Wash me, and I shall be whiter than snow." It originally had six stanzas, all of them beginning, "Dear Jesus . . ." An unknown editor later altered the words to "Lord Jesus." "Whiter Than Snow" was first published in 1872 by the Methodist Episcopal Book Room in Philadelphia, in a sixteen-page pamphlet entitled *Joyful Songs No. 4.*

Philadelphia musician William Gustavus Fischer composed the music to this hymn. He learned to read music while attending singing classes at a German-speaking church in Philadelphia. When he started his life's occupation as a bookbinder, he still spent his evenings pursuing music. He was eventually hired to teach music at a Philadelphia college, and late in life he entered the piano business.

Fischer was best known as a popular song leader for revival meetings. In 1875, he led the thousand-voice choir at the D.L. Moody / Ira Sankey Campaign in the great tabernacle at Thirteenth and Market Streets in Philadelphia. He composed more than two hundred hymn tunes, including this one. He also composed the melody for "I Love to Tell the Story."

The splendor of snowfall is only one of the pictures used in Scripture to illustrate God's forgiveness of sin. Micah 7:19 says God casts our sins into the ocean. Psalm 103:12 says He removes them as far from us as east from west. According to Isaiah 38:17, God casts them behind His back. Colossians 2:14 says they are wiped out like erased handwriting. If you're suffering pangs of guilt and regret, needing a fresh experience of God's forgiveness, try singing this old hymn with new sincerity:

*Break down every idol, cast out every foe.*
*Now wash me and I shall be whiter than snow.*

## VERSE OF THE WEEK

Wash me, and I shall be whiter than snow.

—Psalm 51:7

# REFLECT

Consider David's prayer of repentance after his sin with Bathsheba (Psalm 51:7). How might he have felt in that moment?

_____

_____

_____

_____

_____

This song about repentance was written by a committed, dedicated Christian. Consider Romans 3:23. What does it say about sin?

_____

_____

_____

_____

The hymn offers an assurance in this line: "To those who have sought Thee / Thou never saidst, 'No.'" Who is someone special you hope will come to salvation in Christ? Lift up a prayer for them right now.

_____

_____

_____

The passage lists several word pictures used in Scripture to illustrate God's forgiveness of sin. Which appeals to you most and why?

_____

_____

_____

*Make Thou my spirit pure and clear*
*As are the frosty skies,*
*Or this first snowdrop of the year*
*That in my bosom lies.*
      —ALFRED, LORD TENNYSON (1809–1892)

*Amen.*

## PRAYER REQUESTS FOR THE WEEK

_____

_____

# Immortal, Invisible, God Only Wise

Walter Chalmers Smith

Welsh Hymn Melody

# IMMORTAL, INVISIBLE, GOD ONLY WISE

1876

The city of Edinburgh, Scotland, with its Royal Mile and rugged hilltop castle, has produced some of Christianity's greatest hymnists: George Matheson ("O Love That Wilt Not Let Me Go"), Horatius Bonar ("I Heard the Voice of Jesus Say"), Elizabeth Clephane ("Beneath the Cross of Jesus"), and William Mackay ("Revive Us Again"), to name a few. And who but the sturdy Scotch Presbyterians could produce such a powerful hymn on the sovereign, eternal power of God as "Immortal, Invisible, God Only Wise"?

The author, Walter Chalmers Smith, was born in Aberdeen on December 5, 1824. After attending grammar school at the University of Aberdeen, he enrolled in New College, Edinburgh, and was ordained as a minister in the Free Church of Scotland in 1850. He pastored churches in several places, including the lovely Scottish village of Milnathort from 1853 to 1858.

In 1874, he became pastor of the Free High Church (Presbyterian) of Edinburgh, a charge he kept until his retirement in 1894.[5] Two years into his pastorate, he published a collection of hymns titled *Hymns of Christ and the Christian Life*. It was here that "Immortal, Invisible, God Only Wise" was introduced to the world.

Walter Smith was blessed with two other honors. In 1893, he was elected Moderator of the Free Church of Scotland. And in 1902, a collection of his poetry was published. His poems reflect his Scottish nature and remind us of Robert Burns. A number of them had appeared in various publications over the years, published under the pseudonyms "Orwell" and "Herman Knott." One of his best-known poems, "Glenaradale," begins:

> *There is no fire of the crackling boughs / On the hearth of our fathers,*
> *There is no lowing of brown-eyed cows / On the green meadows,*
> *Nor do the maidens whisper vows / In the still gloaming,*
> *Glenaradale.*

"Immortal, Invisible, God Only Wise" was based on 1 Timothy 1:17. It was originally published in six stanzas. When the hymn was republished in 1884, Smith made a few alterations. Today's version uses Smith's first three stanzas, and the fourth stanza is pieced together from lines in the now-discarded verses.

The powerful melody is called St. Denio and is based on a Welsh folk song.

Now to the King eternal, immortal, invisible, to God who alone is wise, be honor and glory forever and ever. Amen.

—1 TIMOTHY 1:17

# REFLECT

· · · · · · · · · · · · · · · · · · · · · · · · · · · · · · · · · · · · · · · · · · · · ·

This hymn borrows its title from 1 Timothy 1:17. It highlights three powerful attributes of God: immortal, invisible, only wise. What do these words indicate about the character of God?

_____

_____

_____

_____

_____

This hymn calls God "the Ancient of Days." This name for God is used in Daniel 7 and points to God's eternal nature. Why do you think the author used that name for God here?

_____

_____

_____

_____

_____

The theme of this hymn is the sovereignty and power of God. On a personal level, how does God's sovereignty give you hope?

_____

_____

_____

Verse three invites us to pay special attention to God as a source of life. Make note of how God gives life to something or someone "great." Now note God's life in something "small."

_____

_____

_____

*Help us, O God, to serve Thee devoutly and the world busily. May we do our work wisely, give succour secretly, go to our meat appetitely, sit thereat discreetly, arise temperately, please our friend duly, go to our bed merrily and sleep surely, for the joy of our Lord Jesus Christ. Amen.*
—SULPICIUS SEVERUS (C. 363–C. 420)

## PRAYER REQUESTS FOR THE WEEK

_____

_____

# Moment by Moment

Daniel W. Whittle

May W. Moody

1. Dy-ing with Je - sus, by death reck-oned mine, Liv-ing with Je - sus a
2. Nev-er a tri - al that He is not there, Nev-er a bur-den that
3. Nev-er a heart-ache, and nev-er a groan, Nev-er a tear-drop and
4. Nev-er a weak-ness that He doth not feel, Nev-er a sick-ness that

new life di - vine, Look-ing to Je-sus 'til glo-ry doth shine, Mo-ment by
He doth not bear, Nev - er a sor-row that He doth not share, Mo-ment by
nev - er a moan; Nev - er a dan-ger but there on the throne, Mo-ment by
He can-not heal; Mo-ment by mo-ment, in woe or in weal, Je - sus, my

mo-ment, O Lord, I am Thine.
mo-ment, I'm un - der His care.
mo-ment, He thinks of His own. Mo-ment by mo-ment I'm kept in His love,
Sav - ior, a - bides with me still.

Mo-ment by mo-ment I've life from a - bove; Look-ing to Je-sus 'til

glo-ry doth shine, Mo - ment by mo-ment, O Lord, I am Thine.

# MOMENT BY MOMENT

1893

Much of our information about the hymns of the gospel song era comes from *My Life and the Story of the Gospel Hymns* by Ira Sankey, the "singing evangelist," who accompanied D.L. Moody around the world.[6] Here's what he said about this enduring hymn:

"While I was attending the World's Fair in Chicago, Henry Varley, a lay preacher from London, said to Major Daniel Whittle: 'I do not like the hymn, "I Need Thee Every Hour," very well, because I need Him every moment of the day.' Soon after Major Whittle wrote this sweet hymn, having the chorus:

> *Moment by moment I'm kept in His love;*
> *Moment by moment I've life from above;*
> *Looking to Jesus till glory doth shine;*
> *Moment by moment, O Lord, I am Thine.*

"Mr. Whittle brought the hymn to me in manuscript a little later, saying that he would give me the copyright of both the words and music if I would print for him five hundred copies on fine paper, for distribution among his friends. His daughter, May Whittle, who later became the wife of Will R. Moody, composed the music. I did as Mr. Whittle wished; and I sent the hymn to England, where it was copyrighted on the same day as in Washington.

"In England, the hymn became very popular. Falling into the hands of the well-known Rev. Andrew Murray, of South Africa, then visiting London, he adopted it as his favorite hymn. A year later Mr. Murray visited Northfield, and while holding a meeting for men in the church he remarked, 'If Mr. Sankey only knew a hymn which I found in London, and would sing it; he would find that it embraces my entire creed.'

"I was very anxious to know what hymn it was, and when he had recited it, I said to him, 'Doctor, that hymn was written within five hundred yards of where we are standing.'"

## VERSE OF THE WEEK

Praise be to the Lord, to God our Savior, who daily bears our burdens.

—Psalm 68:19 (niv)

## REFLECT

· · · · · · · · · · · · · · · · · · · · · · · · · · · · · · · · · · · ·

We know the origins of this song because of the first-person account from Ira Sankey in his book *My Life and the Story of the Gospel Hymns.* After reading the endnote to this passage (see note 6 on page 211), what do you think about Sankey's determination to complete that publication?

The hymn highlights our dependence on Jesus, past, present, and future ("dying with Jesus," "living with Jesus," and "looking to Jesus"). How are you depending on Jesus today?

Verse two highlights Jesus as a source of comfort during trials, burdens, and sorrows. What does Jesus promise in Matthew 5:4 about those who are suffering?

_____

_____

_____

Verse three reminds us that Jesus understands heartache and sorrow. Think about a time when you felt sorrow overwhelming you, then read Matthew 26:38. How does it make you feel to know Jesus understands?

_____

_____

_____

> *Jesus Christ my God, I adore You and I thank You for all the graces You have given me this day. I offer You my sleep and all the moments of this night, and I implore You to keep me safe from sin. To this end I place myself in Your sacred side. . . . Let Your holy angels surround me and keep me in peace; and let Your blessing be upon me. Amen.*
> —ALPHONSUS LIGUORI (1696–1787)

## PRAYER REQUESTS FOR THE WEEK

_____

_____

# Nearer, My God, to Thee

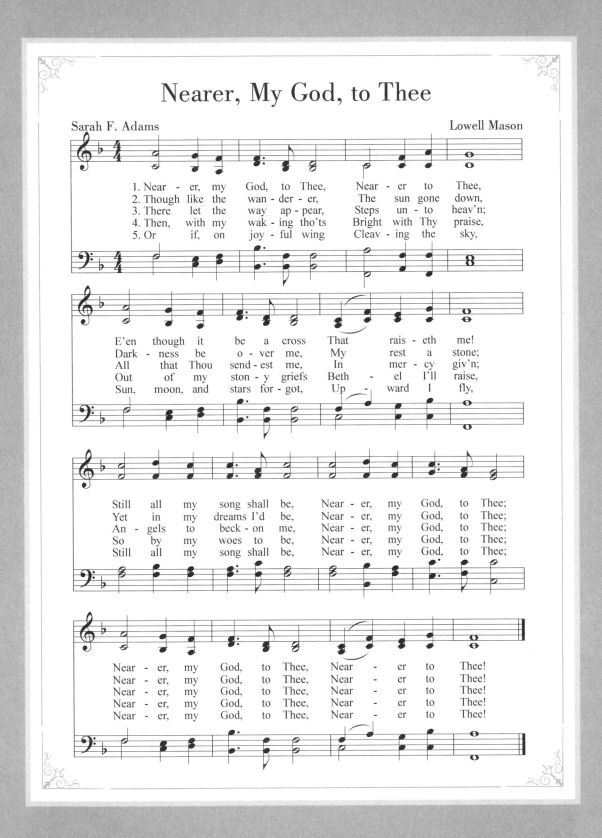

# NEARER, MY GOD, TO THEE

## 1841

It was reported that the band aboard the *Titanic* gallantly played "Nearer, My God, to Thee" as the great liner sank to its watery grave on April 14, 1912. A Canadian survivor told of being comforted by its strains. Historians, however, have never been able to nail down the validity of the story.

Never mind. It's a great hymn anyway, written by a woman named Sarah Flower Adams. She was born in Harlow, England, in the winter of 1805. Her father was a newspaper editor and a man of prominence.

Sarah herself grew up enjoying the spotlight. She showed great interest in the stage and dreamed of being an actress. In 1834, she married William Bridges Adams, a civil engineer. The couple lived in London where Sarah could be near the great theaters. In 1837, she played Lady Macbeth in the Richmond Theatre in London to rave reviews.

Her frail health hampered her career, however, and she found herself focusing more on her literary gifts. It's said that she wrote quickly, as if under compulsion; and seldom did editors find anything to change in her work. Among her compositions were hymns of praise to the Lord. Sarah's sister, Eliza, a gifted musician, often wrote the music for her hymns. The two were very close.

One day in 1841, their pastor, Rev. William Johnson Fox of London's South Place Unitarian Church, paid a visit. He was compiling a church hymnbook and he wanted to include some of their hymns. He further mentioned that he was frustrated at his inability to find a hymn to go along with the upcoming Sunday's message, which was from the story of Jacob at Bethel in Genesis 28:10–22.

Sarah offered to write a hymn based on those verses. For the rest of the week she pored over the passage, visualizing Jacob's sleeping with a stone for his pillow as he dreamed of a ladder reaching to heaven. The following Sunday, South Place Unitarian Church sang Sarah's "Nearer, My God, to Thee."

Eliza, who was suffering from tuberculosis, died in 1846. Sarah had faithfully cared for her sister during the illness, but by the time Eliza died, Sarah, too, was showing signs of consumption.

She passed away on August 14, 1848, at age forty-three.

Then he dreamed, and behold, a ladder was set up on the earth, and its top reached to heaven.

—GENESIS 28:12

# REFLECT

Sarah F. Adams wrote this hymn to accompany a sermon based on Jacob's dream of a ladder reaching heaven. In the lyrics, she doesn't mention a ladder. Rather, what does she imagine (in verse one) lifting her closer to God?

_____

_____

_____

_____

Verse two directly references Jacob with the words "like the wanderer." What is the meaning of "my rest a stone"? How do you relate to feeling that way?

_____

_____

_____

_____

The hymn alludes to Genesis 28:18–22 with the words "Out of my stony griefs / Bethel I'll raise." Why do you think she refers to griefs as "stony"?

_____

_____

_____

What are some ways to increase in nearness to God this side of heaven?

_____

_____

_____

> *O Lord, in Your great mercy, keep us from forgetting what You have suffered for us in body and soul. May we never be drawn by the cares of this life from Jesus our Friend and Savior, but daily may live nearer to His cross. Amen.*
> —CAPTAIN HEDLEY VICARS (1826–1855)

## PRAYER REQUESTS FOR THE WEEK

_____

_____

# Jesus, I Am Resting, Resting

Jean S. Pigott

James Mountain

1. Je - sus, I am rest - ing, rest - ing, In the joy of what Thou art;
2. O, how great Thy lov - ing kind-ness, Vast-er, broad - er than the sea!
3. Sim - ply trust - ing Thee, Lord Je - sus, I be - hold Thee as Thou art,
4. Ev - er lift Thy face up - on me As I work and wait for Thee;

I am find - ing out the great - ness Of Thy lov - ing heart.
O, how mar - ve - lous Thy good - ness, Lav - ished all on me!
And Thy love, so pure, so change-less, Sa - tis - fies my heart;
Rest - ing 'neath Thy smile, Lord Je - sus, Earth's dark sha - dows flee.

Thou hast bid me gaze up - on Thee, And Thy beau - ty fills my soul,
Yes, I rest in Thee, Be - lov - èd, Know what wealth of grace is Thine,
Sa - tis - fies its deep - est long-ings, Meets, sup - plies its ev - ery need,
Bright-ness of my Fa - ther's glo - ry, Sun - shine of my Fa - ther's face,

For by Thy trans - form - ing pow - er, Thou hast made me whole.
Know Thy cer - tain - ty of prom - ise, And have made it mine.
Com - pass-eth me round with bless-ings: Thine is love in - deed!
Keep me ev - er trust - ing, rest - ing, Fill me with Thy grace.

# JESUS, I AM RESTING, RESTING

### 1876

This poem, written by an Irishwoman named Jean Sophia Pigott, became the favorite hymn of J. Hudson Taylor, the great missionary to China. Often, taking a break from his crushing load of work, Hudson would sit at his little reed organ and sing this hymn. It perfectly expressed his greatest life lesson.

Hudson had envisioned a missionary task greater than any since the days of Paul—the evangelization of China. He had established the China Inland Mission in 1865, but it almost proved his undoing. Overwhelmed by worry, work, and responsibility, he was near a breakdown when he received a letter from a fellow missionary, John McCarthy. In it, McCarthy spoke from John 15 about abiding in Christ.

"Abiding, not striving or struggling," wrote McCarthy, "looking off unto Him; trusting Him for present power. . . . This is not new, and yet 'tis new to me. . . . Christ literally all seems to me now the power, the only power for service; the only ground for unchanging joy."

As Hudson read this letter at his mission station in Chin-kiang on Saturday, September 4, 1869, his eyes were opened. "As I read," he recalled, "I saw it all. I looked to Jesus, and when I saw, oh how the joy flowed!"

Writing to his sister in England, he said:

"As to work, mine was never so plentiful, so responsible, or so difficult; but the weight and strain are all gone. The last month or more has been perhaps the happiest of my life, and I long to tell you a little of what the Lord has done for my soul. . . . When the agony of soul was at its height, a sentence in a letter from dear McCarthy was used to remove the scales from my eyes, and the Spirit of God revealed the truth of our oneness with Jesus as I had never known it before. McCarthy, who had been much exercised by the same sense of failure, but saw the light before I did, wrote: 'But how to get faith strengthened? Not by striving after faith but by resting on the Faithful One.'

"As I read, I saw it all! . . . As I thought of the Vine and the branches, what light the blessed Spirit poured into my soul!"

Abide in Me, and I in you. As the branch cannot bear fruit of itself, unless it abides in the vine, neither can you, unless you abide in Me.

—JOHN 15:4

# REFLECT

· · · · · · · · · · · · · · · · · · · · · · · · · · · · · · · · · · · · · · · · · ·

The lyrics of this song were written by poet Jean Sophia Pigott, but the story we read here is about J. Hudson Taylor, a missionary to China, for whom this song was a reminder to "abide, not strive." What does Jesus say about following Him in Matthew 11:30?

_____

_____

_____

_____

What are some ways you can "rest" in Jesus?

_____

_____

_____

_____

_____

_____

Verse three describes how the love of Jesus "satisfies" believers' longings and needs. What is the opposite of satisfaction? How can we address this feeling?

---

---

---

Doodle an image of the truth illustrated by Jesus' words from John 15:4 in the space provided.

> *The day returns and brings me the petty round of irritating concerns and duties. . . . Help me to perform them with laughter and kind face, let cheerfulness abound with industry. Give me to go blithely on my business all this day; bring me to my resting bed weary and content and undishonored; and grant me in the end the gift of sleep. Amen.*
> —ROBERT LOUIS STEVENSON (1850–1894)

## PRAYER REQUESTS FOR THE WEEK

---

---

# Search Me, O God

J. Edwin Orr

Maori Melody

1. Search me, O God, and know my heart to-day;
2. I praise Thee, Lord, for cleans-ing me from sin;
3. Lord, take my life, and make it whol-ly Thine;
4. O Ho-ly Ghost, re-vi-val comes from Thee;

Try me, O Sav-ior, know my thoughts, I pray.
Ful-fill Thy Word, and make me pure with-in.
Fill my poor heart with Thy great love di-vine.
Send a re-vi-val, start the work in me.

See if there be some wick-ed way in me;
Fill me with fire where once I burned with shame;
Take all my will, my pas-sion, self and pride;
Thy Word de-clares Thou wilt sup-ply our need;

Cleanse me from ev-ery sin and set me free.
Grant my de-sire to mag-ni-fy Thy name.
I now sur-ren-der, Lord in me a-bide.
For bless-ings now, O Lord, I hum-bly plead.

Arranged by Mark Hill

# SEARCH ME, O GOD

1936

When I was a student at Columbia International University in South Carolina, a small, peppery, gray-haired Irishman came to lecture. He was brisk and plain-spoken, and his subject was revival. J. Edwin Orr had studied the history of revivals like no one else; as it happened, I had just read one of his many books on the subject.

When I requested an appointment, he agreed to see me in the lobby of the men's dormitory. Perhaps it was his shyness, but he seemed uncomfortable chatting with me. Instead of looking in my direction and engaging in conversation, he gazed straight ahead and answered my questions with short replies. After several fruitless exchanges, I decided to ask him one last thing.

"Dr. Orr, besides praying for revival, what can I do to help bring it about?" Without a moment's pause, he glanced in my direction and gave me an answer I've never forgotten: "You can let it begin with you."

That is exactly the point of this hymn, which he had written years before, in 1936, during an intense springtime revival convention in the town of Ngaruawahia, on the North Island of New Zealand. There had been an attitude of unusual expectancy about the meetings, and prayer meetings proliferated across the city. Many students were coming to Christ, and the area began overflowing with the testimonies of those being saved and renewed in Christ.

One day Dr. Orr heard four Aborigine girls sing a beautiful song entitled "The Song of Farewell," the first words being, "Now is the hour when we must say goodbye." Unable to get the lovely Polynesian tune out of his mind, Dr. Orr began singing it to himself using words from Psalm 139. These words he jotted down on the back of an envelope while standing in the post office at Ngaruawahia, and they were first published in his book *All You Need*.

· · · · · · · · · ·

While this is a wonderful hymn to sing, it is a "dangerous" prayer to offer. We all have sins within us of which we're unaware, for the heart is deceitful above all things. But as we submit ourselves to the searchlight of God's Spirit, we can discover the habits that need to be confessed and the attitudes that need to be changed. As God cleanses us, the result will be revival—one that begins with us.

## VERSE OF THE WEEK

Search me, O God, and know my heart;
Try me, and know my anxieties;
And see if there is any wicked way in me,
And lead me in the way everlasting.

—Psalm 139:23–24

## REFLECT

· · · · · · · · · · · · · · · · · · · · · · · · · · · · · · · · · · · ·

What was Dr. J. Edwin Orr's answer to the question, "Besides prayer, what can I do to help bring about revival?"

_____

_____

_____

_____

_____

The first verse of this hymn is based on Psalm 139:23–24, a prayer of King David. What does God say about David in Acts 13:22?

_____

_____

_____

_____

In what way is this hymn a "dangerous" prayer?

_____

_____

_____

With what does verse two ask God to replace the "burn of shame"?

_____

_____

_____

> *I will extol You, my God, O King;*
> *And I will bless Your name forever and ever.*
> *Every day I will bless You,*
> *And I will praise Your name forever and ever.*
> *Great is the LORD, and greatly to be praised;*
> *And His greatness is unsearchable.*
>
> —PSALM 145:1–3
>
> *Amen.*

## PRAYER REQUESTS FOR THE WEEK

_____

_____

# What a Friend We Have in Jesus

Joseph M. Scriven

Charles C. Converse

1. What a Friend we have in Je-sus, All our sins and griefs to bear!
2. Have we tri-als and temp-ta-tions? Is there trou-ble an-y-where?
3. Are we weak and heav-y-lad-en, Cum-bered with a load of care?

What a priv-i-lege to car-ry, Ev-ery-thing to God in prayer!
We should nev-er be dis-cour-aged; Take it to the Lord in prayer.
Pre-cious Sav-ior, still our ref-uge! Take it to the Lord in prayer.

Oh, what peace we of-ten for-feit, Oh, what need-less pain we bear.
Can we find a friend so faith-ful, Who will all our sor-rows share?
Do Thy friends de-spise, for-sake Thee? Take it to the Lord in prayer.

All be-cause we do not car-ry Ev-ery-thing to God in prayer!
Je-sus knows our ev-ery weak-ness; Take it to the Lord in prayer.
In His arms He'll take and shield Thee; Thou wilt find a so-lace there.

# WHAT A FRIEND WE HAVE IN JESUS

1855

J oseph Scriven watched in shock as the body of his fiancée was pulled from the lake. Their wedding had been planned for the next day. Reeling from the tragedy, he made up his mind to immigrate to America. Packing up his belongings in Dublin, Ireland, he sailed for Canada, leaving his mother behind. He was about twenty-five years old.

Ten years later, in 1855, he received word that his mother was facing a crisis. Joseph wrote this poem and sent it to her. Mrs. Scriven evidently gave a copy to a friend who had it published anonymously, and it quickly became a popular hymn, though no one knew who had written it.

Meanwhile, Joseph fell in love again. But tragedy struck a second time when his fiancée, Eliza Catherine Roche, contracted tuberculosis and died in 1860 before their wedding could take place.

To escape his sorrow, Joseph poured himself into ministry, doing charity work for the Plymouth Brethren and preaching among the Baptists. He lived a simple, obscure life in Port Hope, Canada, cutting firewood for widows and giving away his clothes and money to those in need. He was described as "a man of short stature, with iron-gray hair, close-cropped beard, and light blue eyes that sparkled when he talked." Ira Sankey later wrote:

Until a short time before his death it was not known that he had a poetic gift. A neighbor, sitting up with him in his illness, happened upon a manuscript copy of "What a Friend We Have in Jesus." Reading it with great delight and questioning Mr. Scriven about it, he said that he had composed it for his mother, to comfort her in a time of special sorrow, not intending that anyone else should see it. Some time later, when another Port Hope neighbor asked him if it was true he composed the hymn, his reply was, "The Lord and I did it between us."

On October 10, 1896, Joseph became critically ill. In his delirium, he rose from his bed and staggered outdoors where he fell into a small creek and drowned at age sixty-six. His grave was arranged so that his feet were opposite those of his lost love, Eliza Catherine Roche, that at the resurrection they might arise facing one another.

The peace of God, which surpasses all understanding,
will guard your hearts and minds through Christ Jesus.

—PHILIPPIANS 4:7

# REFLECT

Joseph M. Scriven wrote this song for his mother when she was facing a crisis. What have you written before intending to encourage a loved one?

_____

_____

_____

_____

_____

What does the passage say Scriven did to "escape his sorrow"? Do you think this is a typical reaction? Why or why not?

_____

_____

_____

_____

_____

This hymn reminds us of the "privilege" of bringing "everything" to God in prayer, which is easier said than done. What do we often leave off bringing to God and why?

_____

_____

_____

What does Philippians 4:6–7 say about bringing our requests to God?

_____

_____

_____

> *What a good friend You are, Lord! You are so patient, willing to wait as long as necessary for me to turn to You. You rejoice at the times when I love You, but You do not hold against me the times when I ignore You. Your patience is beyond my understanding. Even when I pray, my mind fills with worldly concerns and vain daydreams. Yet You are happy if I give only a second of honest prayer, turning that second into a seed of love. O Lord, I enjoy Your friendship so much. . . . Amen.*
> —TERESA OF ÁVILA (1515–1582)

## PRAYER REQUESTS FOR THE WEEK

_____

_____

# Take Time to Be Holy

William D. Longstaff

George C. Stebbins

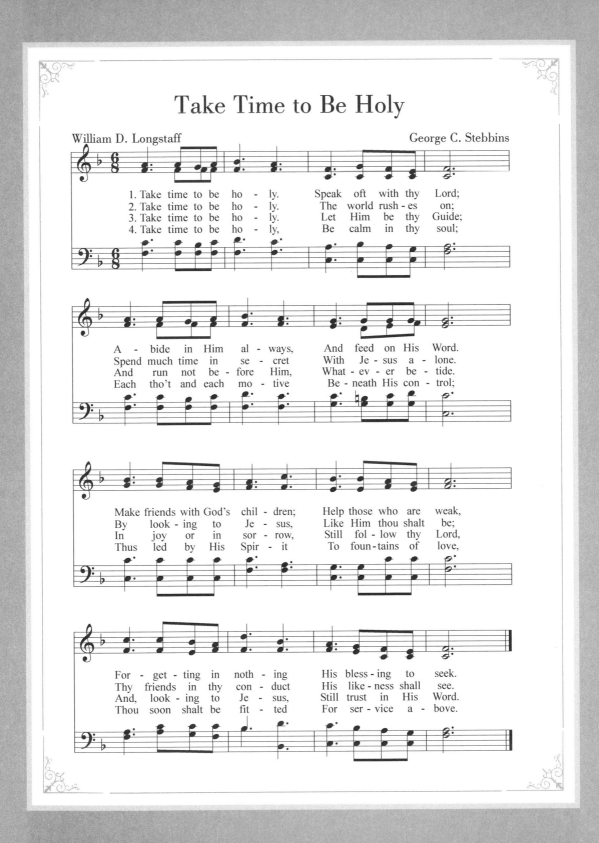

1. Take time to be ho - ly. Speak oft with thy Lord;
2. Take time to be ho - ly. The world rush - es on;
3. Take time to be ho - ly. Let Him be thy Guide;
4. Take time to be ho - ly, Be calm in thy soul;

A - bide in Him al - ways, And feed on His Word.
Spend much time in se - cret With Je - sus a - lone.
And run not be - fore Him, What - ev - er be - tide.
Each tho't and each mo - tive Be - neath His con - trol;

Make friends with God's chil - dren; Help those who are weak,
By look - ing to Je - sus, Like Him thou shalt be;
In joy or in sor - row, Still fol - low thy Lord,
Thus led by His Spir - it To foun - tains of love,

For - get - ting in noth - ing His bless - ing to seek.
Thy friends in thy con - duct His like - ness shall see.
And, look - ing to Je - sus, Still trust in His Word.
Thou soon shalt be fit - ted For ser - vice a - bove.

# TAKE TIME TO BE HOLY

### 1882

The words to "Take Time to Be Holy" were written about 1882 by William Longstaff, a wealthy Englishman who served as treasurer of the Bethesda Free Chapel in Sunderland, a port city in North East England. His church hosted the first meetings held by D.L. Moody and Ira Sankey in that area, and Longstaff became a great supporter of the two.

In his book of hymn stories, Ira Sankey said that "Take Time to Be Holy" was prompted by a sermon William heard in New Brighton on the text "Be holy, for I am holy" (1 Peter 1:16). George C. Stebbins, who composed the music, said Longstaff was inspired to write this poem after hearing a missionary to China quoted as saying, "Take time to be holy." There's no reason why both stories can't be true.

. . . . . . . . .

The tune, HOLINESS, was composed by George C. Stebbins, who cast a long shadow over gospel music. In his book, *Reminiscences and Gospel Hymn Stories*, Stebbins told of his travels and ministries with people like D. L. Moody, Major Daniel Whittle, Philip P. Bliss, Ira Sankey, William Doane, and Fanny Crosby.

In 1890, Stebbins spent time in India working with evangelist George Pentecost. Someone mentioned the need for a hymn on holiness. Stebbins had a habit of making notebooks of poems and hymns by cutting and pasting.[7] Searching through his pages, he found a poem previously clipped and saved—Longstaff's "Take Time to Be Holy." He composed music for the stanzas and sent the words and music to Ira Sankey in New York where it was published. This hymn has not only aged well; it has become more and more relevant. If people in the 1880s needed to slow down and be holy, how much more now!

George Stebbins aged well too. He lived to be nearly one hundred years old, dying in 1945. When he was ninety-five, living in a house in the Catskills, he received a visit from George Beverly Shea, who was just beginning the ministry of sacred song. Shea later described him as hard of hearing but alert, "a tall man with whiskers" who "exuded great dignity and warmth."

Shea was persuaded to sing for the old man, but he had to sing loudly—and right into his ear.

## VERSE OF THE WEEK

It is written, "Be holy, for I am holy."
—1 Peter 1:16

## REFLECT

The author writes, "If people in the 1880s needed to slow down and be holy, how much more now!" Do you agree? Why or why not?

_____

_____

_____

_____

_____

How can we help each other heed the counsel of this song?

_____

_____

_____

_____

_____

How can you "feed on His Word" this week?

_____

_____

_____

Verse three cautions us to "run not before Him." What does this mean to you? How might we avoid this?

_____

_____

_____

> *Keep us, O God, from all pettiness, let us be large in thought, in word, in deed. . . . Let us take time for all things, and make us to grow calm, serene, and gentle. Teach us to put into action our better impulses, straightforward and unafraid. Grant that we may realize that it is the little things of life that create differences, that in the big things of life, we are as one. And, O Lord God, let us not forget to be kind! Amen.*
> —Mary Stuart, Queen of Scotland (1542–1587)

## PRAYER REQUESTS FOR THE WEEK

_____

_____

# I Must Tell Jesus

Elisha A. Hoffman

Elisha A. Hoffman

1. I must tell Je - sus All of my tri - als, I can - not bear These
2. I must tell Je - sus All of my trou - bles, He is a kind, Com -
3. O how the world to e - vil al - lures me. O how my heart Is

bur - dens a - lone. In my dis - tress He kind - ly will help me.
pas - sion - ate friend. If I but ask Him, He will de - liv - er,
tempt - ed to sin. I must tell Je - sus And He will help me,

He ev - er loves And cares for His own. I must tell Je - sus!
Make of my trou - bles Quick - ly an end. I must tell Je - sus!
O - ver the world The vic - t'ry to win.

I must tell Je - sus! I can - not bear My bur - dens a - lone.

I must tell Je - sus! I must tell Je - sus! Je - sus can help me, Je - sus a - lone.

# I MUST TELL JESUS

1894

Many New Testament promises have corresponding verses in the Old Testament that reinforce their power. When Peter, for example, said, "Therefore humble yourselves under the mighty hand of God, that He may exalt you in due time, casting all your care upon Him, for He cares for you" (1 Peter 5:6–7), he was but restating David's words in Psalm 55:22: "Cast your burden on the LORD, and He shall sustain you; He shall never permit the righteous to be moved."

Elisha A. Hoffman loved those verses. He was born May 7, 1839, in Orwigsburg, Pennsylvania. His father was a minister, and Elisha followed Christ at a young age. He attended Philadelphia public schools, studied science, then pursued the classics at Union Seminary of the Evangelical Association. He worked for eleven years with the association's publishing house in Cleveland, Ohio. Then, following the death of his young wife, he returned to Pennsylvania and devoted thirty-three years to pastoring Benton Harbor Presbyterian Church.

Hoffman's pastime was writing hymns, many of which were inspired by pastoral incidents. One day, for example, while calling on the destitute of Lebanon, Pennsylvania, he met a woman whose depression seemed beyond cure. She opened her heart and poured on him her pent-up sorrows. Wringing her hands, she cried, "What shall I do? Oh, what shall I do?" Hoffman knew what she should do, for he had himself learned the deeper lessons of God's comfort. He said to the woman, "You cannot do better than to take all your sorrows to Jesus. You must tell Jesus."

Suddenly the lady's face lit up. "Yes!" she cried. "That's it! I must tell Jesus." Her words echoed in Hoffman's ears, and he mulled them over as he returned home. He drew out his pen and started writing:

*I must tell Jesus! I must tell Jesus!*
*I cannot bear my burdens alone;*
*I must tell Jesus! I must tell Jesus!*
*Jesus can help me, Jesus alone.*

Hoffman lived to be ninety, telling Jesus his burdens and giving the church such hymns as "What a Wonderful Savior," "Down at the Cross," "Are You Washed in the Blood?," "Leaning on the Everlasting Arms," and a thousand more.[8]

Cast your burden on the LORD,
And He shall sustain you;
He shall never permit the righteous to be moved.

—PSALM 55:22

# REFLECT

What question did the woman ask Elisha A. Hoffman that inspired him to write this song? Have you ever asked this question?

_____

_____

_____

_____

_____

What was troubling the woman? Have you ever experienced anything like this?

_____

_____

_____

_____

_____

In verse two we sing, "If I but ask Him / He will deliver." Write down the words of Jesus in John 14:13–14.

_____

_____

_____

Why does 1 Peter 5:7 say we should give our worries and cares to God?

_____

_____

_____

*Sweet and loving God, when I stay asleep too long, oblivious to all Your many blessings, then, please, wake me up, and sing to me Your joyful song. It is a song without noise or notes. It is a song of love beyond words, of faith beyond the power of human telling. I can hear it in my soul, when You awaken me to Your presence. Amen.*
—MECHTHILD OF MAGDEBURG (C. 1207–C. 1290)

## PRAYER REQUESTS FOR THE WEEK

_____

_____

# Sweet Hour of Prayer

Attr. to William W. Walford

William B. Bradbury

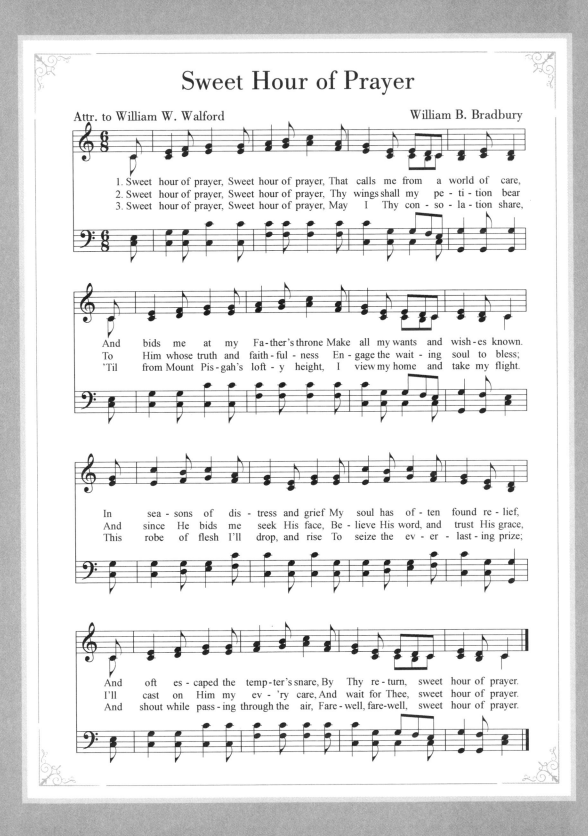

1. Sweet hour of prayer, Sweet hour of prayer, That calls me from a world of care,
2. Sweet hour of prayer, Sweet hour of prayer, Thy wings shall my pe-ti-tion bear
3. Sweet hour of prayer, Sweet hour of prayer, May I Thy con-so-la-tion share,

And bids me at my Fa-ther's throne Make all my wants and wish-es known.
To Him whose truth and faith-ful-ness En-gage the wait-ing soul to bless;
'Til from Mount Pis-gah's loft-y height, I view my home and take my flight.

In sea-sons of dis-tress and grief My soul has of-ten found re-lief,
And since He bids me seek His face, Be-lieve His word, and trust His grace,
This robe of flesh I'll drop, and rise To seize the ev-er-last-ing prize;

And oft es-caped the temp-ter's snare, By Thy re-turn, sweet hour of prayer.
I'll cast on Him my ev-'ry care, And wait for Thee, sweet hour of prayer.
And shout while pass-ing through the air, Fare-well, fare-well, sweet hour of prayer.

# SWEET HOUR OF PRAYER

### 1845

"Sweet Hour of Prayer" first appeared in the *New York Observer* on September 13, 1845, accompanied by this explanatory note by a Rev. Thomas Salmon, a British minister recently immigrated to America:

> At Coleshill, Warwickshire, England, I became acquainted with W.W. Walford, the blind preacher, a man of obscure birth and connections and no education, but of strong mind and most retentive memory. In the pulpit he never failed to select a lesson well adapted to his subject, giving chapter and verse with unerring precision and scarcely ever misplacing a word in his repetition of the Psalms, every part of the New Testament, the prophecies, and some of the histories, so as to have the reputation of "knowing the whole Bible by heart." He actually sat in the chimney corner, employing his mind in composing a sermon or two for Sabbath delivery. . . . On one occasion, paying him a visit, he repeated two or three pieces he had composed, and having no friend at home to commit them to paper, he had laid them up in the storehouse within. "How will this do?" asked he, as he repeated the following lines. . . . I rapidly copied the lines with my pencil as he uttered them, and sent them for insertion in the *Observer*.

No one, however, has ever found a trace of a blind preacher named W.W. Walford in Coleshill, England. There was a Congregational minister named William Walford who wrote a book about prayer containing striking similarities to this poem, and some believe he was the author. But he was neither blind nor uneducated, and the authorship of this hymn remains a mystery.

There's yet another mystery—a deeper one—connected with this hymn. It's the question Jesus asked Simon Peter in Gethsemane: "What? Could you not watch with Me one hour?" If an hour spent with the Lord is so sweet, why do we race through our day prayerless, then squeeze all our requests into a two-minute segment at bedtime? If prayer is so powerful, why do we neglect it so consistently? An oft-omitted verse to this hymn says:

> *Sweet hour of prayer! Sweet hour of prayer! / The joys I feel, the bliss I share,*
> *Of those whose anxious spirits burn / With strong desires for thy return!*
> *With such I hasten to the place / Where God my Savior shows His face,*
> *And gladly take my station there, / And wait for thee, sweet hour of prayer!*

Hear my cry, O God;
Attend to my prayer.

—Psalm 61:1

# REFLECT

· · · · · · · · · · · · · · · · · · · · · · · · · · · · · · · · · ·

What do you consistently spend one hour doing each day?

_____

_____

_____

_____

_____

_____

The Gospels give us many examples of Jesus spending extended stretches of time in prayer. What kept Peter from prayer in Matthew 26:40?

_____

_____

_____

_____

_____

What do you think about the question the author asks: "If prayer is so powerful, why do we neglect it so consistently?"

_____

_____

_____

Some Christians observe set prayer times throughout the day. Try setting your alarm to remind you to pray several times today. What hurdles might stand in the way of accomplishing this?

_____

_____

_____

> _Good Shepherd Jesus, good, gentle, tender Shepherd . . . I ask You, by the power of Your most sweet name, and by Your holy manhood's mystery, to put away my sins and heal the languors of my soul, mindful only of Your goodness, not of my ingratitude. Lord, may Your good, sweet Spirit descend into my heart, and fashion there a dwelling for Himself. Amen._
>
> —AELRED OF RIEVAULX (C. 1110–1167)

## PRAYER REQUESTS FOR THE WEEK

_____

_____

# All Creatures of Our God and King

St. Francis of Assisi

*Geistliche Kirchengesänge* Cologne

1. All   crea-tures of  our God and   King,      Lift     up your voice and with us
2. Let     all  things their Cre - a - tor    bless,      And    wor-ship Him in hum-ble-

sing,    Al -le - lu - ia!  Al -le - lu - ia!  Thou    burn-ing  sun  with
ness.     O    praise Him!  Al -le - lu - ia!  Praise,  praise the  Fa - ther,

gold - en    beam,   Thou  sil - ver moon with soft-er gleam,    O  praise Him
praise the    Son,    And  praise the  spir - it, Three in One!    O  praise Him

O    praise Him! Al-le - lu - ia!  Al-le - lu - ia!  Al-le - lu  -  ia!

# ALL CREATURES OF OUR GOD AND KING

## 1225

So many stories have arisen around St. Francis of Assisi that it's difficult to separate truth from fiction. We know he was born in 1182 in central Italy, the son of a rich merchant. After a scanty education, Francis joined the army and was captured in war. He came to Christ shortly after his release, renounced his wealth, and began traveling about the countryside, preaching the gospel, living simply, seeking to make Christ real to everyone he met.

Francis loved nature, and many stories spotlight his interaction with animals. Once as he hiked through Italy's Spoleto Valley, he came upon a flock of birds. When they didn't fly away, he decided to preach them a little sermon: "My brother and sister birds," he reportedly said, "you should praise your Creator and always love Him. He gave you feathers for clothes, wings to fly, and all other things you need. It is God who made your home in thin, pure air. Without sowing or reaping, you receive God's guidance and protection."

The flock, it is said, then flew off rejoicing.

That perspective is reflected in a hymn Francis composed just before his death in 1225, called "Cantico di fratre sole"—"Song of Brother Sun." It exhorts all creation to worship God. The sun and moon. All the birds. All the clouds. Wind and fire. All men of tender heart. All creatures of our God and King.

Though the hymn was written in 1225, an English version didn't appear until 1919, when Rev. William H. Draper decided to use it for a children's worship festival in Leeds, England.

But is it sound theology to exhort birds and billowing clouds to lift their voices in praise? Yes! "All Creatures of our God and King" simply restates an older hymn—Psalm 148—which says:

> *Praise Him, sun and moon; / Praise Him, all you stars of light! . . . /*
> *You great sea creatures and all the depths; / Fire and hail, snow and clouds; /*
> *Stormy wind, fulfilling His word; / Mountains and all hills; /*
> *Fruitful trees and all cedars; / Beasts and all cattle; /*
> *Creeping things and flying fowl. . . . / Let them praise the name of the LORD, /*
> *For His name alone is exalted. . . . / Praise the LORD!*

I tell you that if these should keep silent, the stones would immediately cry out.

—LUKE 19:40

# REFLECT

· · · · · · · · · · · · · · · · · · · · · · · · · · · · · · · · · · · · ·

What did you think of the story about St. Francis preaching to a flock of birds?

_____

_____

_____

_____

_____

_____

Who and/or what is being asked to praise God in Psalm 148?

_____

_____

_____

_____

_____

_____

Who and/or what is being asked to praise God in St. Francis's lyrics?

_____

_____

_____

How does singing this song make you feel?

_____

_____

_____

*Father, light up the small duties of this day; may they shine with the beauty of Your face. May I believe that glory can dwell in the commonest task every day. Amen.*
—AUGUSTINE OF HIPPO (354–430)

## PRAYER REQUESTS FOR THE WEEK

_____

_____

# Praise Ye the Lord, the Almighty

Joachim Neander                                    *Straslund Gesangbuch*

1. Praise to the Lord, the Al - might - y, The King of cre - a - tion!
2. Praise to the Lord, Who o'er all things So won-drous-ly reign - eth,
3. Praise to the Lord! O let all that is in me a - dore Him!
4. Praise to the Lord, Who doth pros - per Thy work and de - fend thee;

O my soul, praise Him, For He is thy health and sal - va - tion!
Shel - ters thee un - der His wings, Yes, so gent - ly sus - tain - eth!
All that hath life and breath, Come now with prais - es be - fore Him.
Sure - ly His good - ness and mer - cy Here dail - y at - tend thee.

All ye who hear,          Now to His tem - ple draw near;
Hast Thou not seen        How all thy long - ings have been
Let the a - men           sound from His peo - ple a - gain:
Pon - der a - new          what the Al - might - y can do,

Join me in glad ad - o - ra - tion!
Grant - ed in what He or - dain - eth?
Glad - ly for aye we a - dore Him.
If with His love He be - friend thee.

# PRAISE YE THE LORD, THE ALMIGHTY

1680

This hymn was written by Joachim Neander, born in 1650, whose father, grandfather, great-grandfather, and great-great-grandfather—all Joachim Neanders—had been preachers of the gospel. But as a student, Joachim was wild and rebellious. At twenty, he joined a group of students who descended on St. Martin's Church in Bremen to ridicule and scoff at the worshippers. But the sermon that day by Rev. Theodore Under-Eyck arrested him and led to his conversion. A few years later, he was the assistant preacher at that very church.

Joachim often took long walks near his home in Hochdal, Germany. They were worship walks, and he frequently composed hymns as he strolled, singing them to the Lord. He was the first hymnwriter from the Calvinist branch of Protestantism. When he was thirty—the year he died—he wrote this while battling tuberculosis:

> *Praise ye the Lord, the Almighty, the King of creation.*
> *O my soul, praise Him, for He is thy health and salvation.*

One of Joachim's favorite walking spots was a beautiful gorge a few miles from Dusseldorf. The Dussel River flowed through the valley, and Joachim Neander so loved this spot that it eventually was named for him—Neander Valley. The Old German word for "valley" was *tal* or *thal* with a silent *h*.

Two hundred years later Herr von Beckersdorf owned the valley, which was a source for limestone, used to manufacture cement. In 1856, miners discovered caves that contained human bones. Beckersdorf took the bones to a local science teacher who speculated they belonged to one who died in the Flood.

But when William King, an Irish professor of anatomy, saw the bones, he claimed they were proof of evolution's famous "missing link." Other Neanderthal fossils were found, and for many years they were used to "prove" Darwin's theory of evolution. Today we know the Neanderthal was fully human, an extinct people group of great strength.

But, as one expert put it, "when Joachim Neander walked in his beautiful valley so many years ago, he could not know that hundreds of years later his name would become world famous, not for his hymns celebrating creation, but for a concept that he would have totally rejected: human evolution."[9]

Where were you when I laid the foundations of the earth? Tell Me, if you have understanding.

—Job 38:4

# REFLECT

· · · · · · · · · · · · · · · · · · · · · · · · · · · · · · · · · · · · · · · · · ·

The author of this hymn, Joachim Neander, died of tuberculosis when he was just thirty. Why might it be said that God is the soul's "health"?

What do you think of the irony of the Neanderthal story cited in this passage? How do you see God's ways at work in this?

See Psalm 150:6. What line of the hymn corresponds to this verse?

_____

_____

_____

Take a moment to "ponder anew what the Almighty can do." Make a note of any thoughts that occur to you.

_____

_____

_____

> *I beseech Thee, Almighty God, to purify my conscience by Thy daily visitation, that when Your Son Jesus Christ my Lord comes He may find in me a mansion swept clean, prepared for Himself; who lives and reigns with Thee and the Holy Spirit, One God, now and forever. Amen.*
> —GELASIAN SACRAMENTARY (8TH C.)

## PRAYER REQUESTS FOR THE WEEK

_____

_____

# O Worship the King

Robert Grant

Johann Michael Haydn

1. O wor-ship the King, All glo-rious a-bove, And
2. O tell of His might, And sing of His grace, Whose
3. Thy boun-ti-ful care, What tongue can re-cite? It
4. Frail child-ren of dust, And fee-ble as frail, In

grate-ful-ly sing His power and His love: Our
robe is the light, His Whose can-o-py space. His
breathes in the air; It shines in the light. It
Thee do we trust, Nor find Thee to fail. Thy

Shield and De-fend-er, The An-cient of Days, Pa-
char-iots of wrath, The deep thun-der-clouds form, And
streams from the hills; It de-scends to the plain, And
mer-cies how ten-der! How firm to the end! Our

vil-ioned in splen-dor, And gird-ed with praise.
dark is His path On the wings of the storm.
sweet-ly dis-tills In the dew and the rain.
Mak-er, De-fend-er, Re-deem-er, and Friend!

# O WORSHIP THE KING

1833

Charles Grant, director of the East India Company, was respected throughout India as one of Britain's finest statesmen. He was also a deeply committed Christian, an evangelical in the Anglican Church, who used his position in India to encourage missionary expansion there.

In 1778, just as England was reeling from the American Revolution, Charles returned to the British Isles to become a Member of Parliament from Inverness, Scotland. His son, Robert, six years old at the time, grew up in a world of power, politics, and privilege. But he also grew up as a devout and dedicated follower of Christ. As a young man, Robert attended Magdalene College, Cambridge, then entered the legal profession. His intelligence and integrity were obvious. He became King's Serjeant in the Court of the Duchy of Lancaster, and in 1818, he entered Parliament. Among his legislative initiatives was a bill to remove civil restrictions against the Jews.

One day in the early 1830s, as Robert studied Psalm 104, he compared the greatness of the King of kings with the majesty of British royalty. Psalm 104:1 says of God: "O LORD my God, You are very great: You are clothed with honor and majesty." Verses 2–3 add that God covers Himself "with light as with a garment" and "makes the clouds His chariot." Verse 5 reminds us that God "laid the foundations of the earth." All of creation reflects God's greatness, verse 24 proclaiming, "O LORD, how manifold are Your works!" Verse 31 says, "May the glory of the LORD endure forever."

Robert filled his heart with these verses, and from his pen came one of the most magnificent hymns in Christendom:

> *O worship the King, all glorious above,*
> *And gratefully sing His power and His love:*
> *Our Shield and Defender, the Ancient of Days,*
> *Pavilioned in splendor, and girded with praise.*

In 1832, Robert was appointed Judge Advocate General; this hymn was published in 1833; and he was knighted in 1834. Soon thereafter, at age fifty, Sir Robert returned to India, land of his early childhood, to be Governor of Bombay. He died there on July 9, 1838. A nearby medical college was built in his honor and named for him. But his most lasting memorial is this majestic hymn of praise, calling us to worship the King of kings.

I will sing to the LORD as long as I live;
I will sing praise to my God while I have my being.

—PSALM 104:33

# REFLECT

. . . . . . . . . . . . . . . . . . . . . . . . . . . . . . . . . . . . .

The passage here points out that Robert Grant was comparing the greatness of God with the majesty of British royalty. Does the idea of God as royalty appeal to you? Why or why not?

_____

_____

_____

_____

Reflect on the imagery of Psalm 104 and compare it to that of this hymn. What images resonate most with you?

_____

_____

_____

_____

The passage calls this hymn "majestic" and "one of the most magnificent" in all Christendom. Do you agree? Why or why not?

_____

_____

_____

Reflect on the final words of the song used to describe God: Maker, Defender, Redeemer, and Friend. How do these words make you feel?

_____

_____

_____

> *O blessed Jesus, give me stillness of soul in Thee. Let Thy mighty calmness reign in me; rule me, O King of Gentleness, King of peace. . . . By Thine own deep patience, give me patience. Make me in this and all things more and more like Thee. Amen.*
>
> —JOHN OF THE CROSS (1542–1591)

## PRAYER REQUESTS FOR THE WEEK

_____

_____

# Crown Him with Many Crowns

Matthew Bridges/Godfrey Thring

George J. Elvey

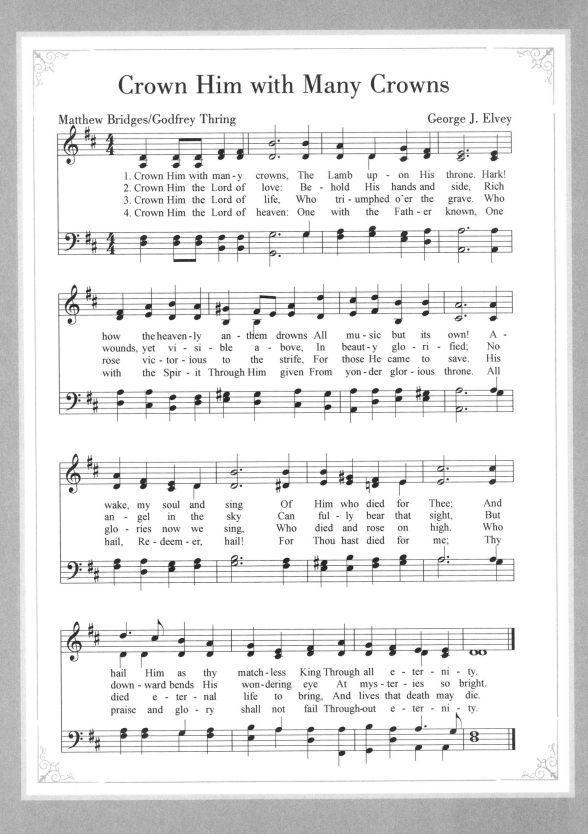

1. Crown Him with man-y crowns, The Lamb up-on His throne. Hark!
2. Crown Him the Lord of love: Be-hold His hands and side, Rich
3. Crown Him the Lord of life, Who tri-umphed o'er the grave. Who
4. Crown Him the Lord of heaven: One with the Fath-er known, One

how the heaven-ly an-them drowns All mu-sic but its own! A-
wounds, yet vi-si-ble a-bove, In beaut-y glo-ri-fied; No
rose vic-tor-ious to the strife, For those He came to save. His
with the Spir-it Through Him given From yon-der glor-ious throne. All

wake, my soul and sing Of Him who died for Thee; And
an-gel in the sky Can ful-ly bear that sight, But
glo-ries now we sing, Who died and rose on high. Who
hail, Re-deem-er, hail! For Thou hast died for me; Thy

hail Him as thy match-less King Through all e-ter-ni-ty.
down-ward bends His won-dering eye At mys-ter-ies so bright.
died e-ter-nal life to bring, And lives that death may die.
praise and glo-ry shall not fail Through-out e-ter-ni-ty.

# CROWN HIM WITH MANY CROWNS

1851

The original form of this hymn was written by Matthew Bridges and consisted of six eight-line stanzas. He thought of his hymn as a sermon in song, based on Revelation 19:12: "And on His head were many crowns." He called his hymn "The Song of the Seraphs." Matthew, who once wrote a book condemning Roman Catholics, ended up converting to Catholicism in 1848. He followed John Henry Newman out of the Church of England.

In 1874, Godfrey Thring, a staunch Anglican clergyman, feared that some of Bridges' verses smacked too much of Catholic doctrine. Verse two, for example, said:

> *Crown Him the virgin's Son, the God incarnate born,*
> *Whose arm those crimson trophies won which now His brow adorn;*
> *Fruit of the mystic rose, as of that rose the stem;*
> *The root whence mercy ever flows, the Babe of Bethlehem.*

It seems odd to us now that such a verse would cause controversy, but in the end Godfrey wrote six new verses for the same song. "Crown Him with Many Crowns" therefore became a six-verse hymn that was written twice!

Over the years, these twelve stanzas have become intermingled in the hymnbooks, with editors mixing and matching the verses. Here are the first lines of all twelve verses, the first six by Bridges, the last six by Thring:

- *Stanza 1: Crown Him with many crowns, the Lamb upon His throne . . .*
- *Stanza 2: Crown Him the virgin's Son, the God incarnate born . . .*
- *Stanza 3: Crown Him the Lord of love, behold His hands and side . . .*
- *Stanza 4: Crown Him the Lord of peace, whose power a scepter sways . . .*
- *Stanza 5: Crown Him the Lord of years, the Potentate of time . . .*
- *Stanza 6: Crown Him the Lord of Heaven, one with the Father known . . .*
- *Stanza 7: Crown Him with crowns of gold . . .*
- *Stanza 8: Crown Him the Son of God, before the worlds began . . .*
- *Stanza 9: Crown Him the Lord of light . . .*
- *Stanza 10: Crown Him the Lord of life, who triumphed over the grave . . .*
- *Stanza 11: Crown Him the Lord of lords, who over all doth reign . . .*
- *Stanza 12: Crown Him the Lord of heaven, enthroned in worlds above . . .*

And on His head were many crowns.

—REVELATION 19:12

# REFLECT

· · · · · · · · · · · · · · · · · · · · · · · · · · · · · · · ·

What Bible verse was this song based on? Using a concordance or online search tool, find other Scripture passages containing the word "crown." How do they inspire you?

_____

_____

_____

_____

_____

The hymn uses a rhetorical device since we can't physically put a crown on Jesus' head. In what way, then, can we "crown Him"?

_____

_____

_____

_____

_____

Do you prefer Godfrey Thring's retooling of the song to make it less controversial? Why or why not?

_____

_____

_____

The line "Awake, my soul" in verse one has an antiquated and yet timeless feel. After waking, what should the soul do next?

_____

_____

_____

> *Praise to God, immortal praise / For the love that crowns our days! . . . / For the blessings of the field, / For the stores the gardens yield . . . / All that liberal Autumn pours / From her rich o'erflowing stores; / Thanks, to Thee, our God, we owe, / Source whence all our blessings flow! / And for these our souls shall raise / Grateful vows and solemn praise.*
> *Amen.*
> —Anna Laetitia Barbauld (1743–1825)

## PRAYER REQUESTS FOR THE WEEK

_____

_____

# Turn Your Eyes Upon Jesus

Helen H. Lemmel                    Helen H. Lemmel

1. O soul, are you wea-ry and trou - bled? No light in the
2. Thro' death in - to life ev - er - last - ing He passed, and we
3. His word shall not fail you He prom - ised; Be - lieve Him, and

dark-ness you see? There's light for a look at the Sav - ior, And
fol - low Him there; O - ver us sin no more hath do - min - ion For
all will be well; Then go to a world that is dy - ing, His

life more a - bun-dant and free!
more than con - qu'rors we are!                Turn your eyes up - on Je - sus,
per - fect sal - va - tion to tell!

Look full in His won - der - ful face,                And the things of

earth Will grow strange-ly dim In the light of His glo - ry and grace.

# TURN YOUR EYES UPON JESUS

1922

Helen Howarth Lemmel was born in England in 1863, into the home of a Wesleyan minister who immigrated to America when Helen was a child. She loved music, and her parents provided the best vocal teachers they could find. Eventually Helen returned to Europe to study vocal music in Germany. In time, she married a wealthy European, but he left her when she became blind, and Helen struggled with multiple heartaches during midlife.

At age fifty-five, Helen heard a statement that deeply impressed her: "So then, turn your eyes upon Him; look full into His face and you will find that the things of earth will acquire a strange new dimness."

"I stood still," Helen later said, "and singing in my soul and spirit was the chorus, with not one conscious moment of putting word to word to make rhyme, or note to note to make melody. The verses were written the same week, after the usual manner of composition, but nonetheless dictated by the Holy Spirit."

Pastor Doug Goins of Palo Alto, California, and his parents, Paul and Kathryn Goins, both eighty-two, of Sun City, Arizona, knew Helen in Seattle. "She was advanced in years and almost destitute, but she was an amazing person," said Doug. "She made a great impression on me as a junior high child because of her joy and enthusiasm. Though she was living on government assistance in a sparse bedroom, whenever we'd ask how she was doing, she would reply, 'I'm doing well in the things that count.'"

One day, the Goins invited her to supper. "We had never entertained a blind person before," recalled Kathryn, "and it was interesting. Despite her infirmities, she was full of life. I remember how amused we were when, following supper, she said, 'Now if you will lead me to the bathroom, I'll sit on the throne and reign.'

"But she was always composing hymns," said Kathryn. "She had no way of writing them down, so she would call my husband at all hours and he'd rush down and record them before she forgot the words."

Helen had a small plastic keyboard by her bed. There she would play, sing, and cry. "One day God is going to bless me with a great heavenly keyboard," she'd say. "I can hardly wait!"

Helen Lemmel, who wrote nearly five hundred hymns during her lifetime, died in Seattle in 1961, thirteen days before her ninety-eighth birthday.

Let us run with endurance the race that is set before us, looking unto Jesus, the author and finisher of our faith.

—Hebrews 12:1–2

# REFLECT

· · · · · · · · · · · · · · · · · · · · · · · · · · · · · · · · · · · · · ·

Helen H. Lemmel, the author of this hymn, was blind. How might that disability have shaped these lyrics?

_____

_____

_____

_____

_____

This hymn was written when the author was fifty-five, after she'd suffered "multiple heartaches." Do you feel the tone of the song is sad or encouraging? Explain as best you can.

_____

_____

_____

_____

How does visually focusing on something affect your mental focus?

_____

_____

_____

Verse one alludes to life "abundant," recalling the words of Jesus. What is Jesus' promise in John 10:10?

_____

_____

_____

> *O Lord God, in whom I live and move and have my being, open my eyes that I may behold Thy fatherly presence ever about me. Draw my heart to Thee with the power of Thy love. Teach me to be anxious for nothing, and when I have done what Thou hast given me to do, help me, O God my Savior, to leave the issue to Thy wisdom. Take from me all doubt and mistrust. Lift my thoughts up to Thee, and make me to know that all things are possible to me through Thy Son my Redeemer. Amen.*
> —BROOKE FOSS WESTCOTT (1825–1901)

## PRAYER REQUESTS FOR THE WEEK

_____

_____

# All Hail the Power of Jesus' Name

# ALL HAIL THE POWER OF JESUS' NAME

1779

In the November 1799 issue of *The Gospel Magazine*, edited by Augustus Toplady, there appeared an anonymous hymn entitled "On the Resurrection, the Lord Is King":

*All hail the power of Jesus' name! Let angels prostrate fall;*
*Bring forth the royal diadem, and crown Him Lord of all.*

The author, it was later revealed, was Rev. Edward Perronet.

Edward's Protestant grandparents had fled Catholic France, going first to Switzerland, then to England. Edward's father had become a vicar in the Anglican Church, and Edward followed in his footsteps.

For several years, he became closely allied with the Wesleys, traveling with them and sometimes caught up in their adventures. In John Wesley's journal, we find this entry: "Edward Perronet was thrown down and rolled in mud and mire. Stones were hurled and windows broken."

In time, however, Edward broke with the Wesleys over various Methodist policies, and John Wesley excluded his hymns from Methodist hymnals. Edward went off to pastor a small independent church in Canterbury, where he died on January 22, 1792. His last words were: "Glory to God in the height of His divinity! Glory to God in the depth of His humanity! Glory to God in His all-sufficiency! Into His hands I commend my spirit."

Edward Perronet's hymn "All Hail the Power" has earned him an indelible place in the history of church music. It also has a place in missionary history, being greatly used in evangelistic endeavors. Rev. E.P. Scott, for example, missionary to India, wrote of trying to reach a savage tribe in the Indian subcontinent. Ignoring the pleadings of his friends, he set off into the dangerous territory. Several days later, he met a large party of warriors who surrounded him, their spears pointed at his heart.

Expecting to die at any moment, Scott took out his violin, breathed a prayer, closed his eyes, and began singing "All Hail the Power of Jesus' Name." When he reached the words "Let every kindred, every tribe," he opened his eyes. There stood the warriors, some in tears, every spear lowered. Scott spent the next two years evangelizing the tribe.

[Jesus Christ] has gone into heaven and is at the right hand of God, angels and authorities and powers having been made subject to Him.

—1 Peter 3:22

# REFLECT

When author Edward Perronet was traveling with the Wesleys, he was attacked. Have you ever suffered injustice because of your faith and witness? How might persecution have influenced his writing?

_____

_____

_____

_____

What does Romans 10:13 say about the name of Jesus?

_____

_____

_____

_____

What does the line "Let angels prostrate fall" mean? What relevance does this hold for you personally?

_____

_____

_____

Who is the "sacred throng" referred to in the final verse?

_____

_____

_____

> *Ere I sleep, for every favour / This day showed / By my God / I will bless my Saviour. / O my Lord, what shall I render / To Thy name, / Still the same, / Merciful and tender? / Thou hast ordered all my goings / In Thy way, / Heard me pray, / Sanctified my doings. . . . / Thou my rock, my guard, my tower, / Safely keep, / While I sleep, / Me, with all Thy power. . . .*
> *Amen.*
>
> —JOHN CENNICK (1718 1755)

## PRAYER REQUESTS FOR THE WEEK

_____

_____

# Rejoice, the Lord Is King

Charles Wesley

John Darwall

1. Re - joice, the Lord is King! Your Lord and King a - dore!
2. Je - sus, the Sav - ior reigns, The God of truth and love;
3. His king-dom can - not fail, He rules o'er earth and heaven;
4. Re - joice in glo - rious hope! Je - sus, the judge shall come,

Mor - tals, give thanks, and sing, And tri-umph ev - er - more:
When He had purged our stains, He took His seat a - bove:
The keys of death and hell Are to our Je - sus given:
And take His ser - vants up To their e - ter - nal home:

Lift up your heart; Lift up your voice!
Lift up your heart; Lift up your voice!
Lift up your heart; Lift up your voice!
Lift up your heart; Lift up your voice!

Re - joice, a - gain I say, re - joice!
Re - joice, a - gain I say, re - joice!
Re - joice, a - gain I say, re - joice!
Re - joice, a - gain I say, re - joice!

# REJOICE, THE LORD IS KING

1744

By the 1740s, Charles Wesley was regularly preaching to thousands in the open air, but opposition was developing. He first encountered physical danger when a doctor in Wales, angry over Charles's sermon, stormed up to him and demanded an apology for having been called a "Pharisee."

Charles, who wasn't known for his tact, replied, "I still insist you are a Pharisee. . . . My commission is to show you your sins, and I shall make no apology for so doing. . . . You are a damned sinner."

The doctor struck Charles with his cane, causing a melee involving several men and women. This was the beginning of a period of dangerous ministry. Here's an entry in Charles's diary from July 22, 1743:

> I had just named my text at St. Ives . . . when an army of rebels broke in upon us. . . . They began in a most outrageous manner, threatening to murder the people, if they did not go out that moment. They broke the sconces, dashed the windows in pieces, tore away the shutters . . . and all but the stone-walls. I stood silently looking on; but mine eyes were unto the Lord. They swore bitterly I should not preach there again; which I disproved, by immediately telling them Christ died for them all. Several times they lifted up their hands and clubs to strike me; but a stronger arm restrained them. They beat and dragged the women about, particularly one of a great age, and trampled on them without mercy. The longer they stayed, and the more they raged, the more power I found from above. . . .

It was during these days of danger that Charles wrote his triumphant hymn "Rejoice, the Lord Is King," the third verse of which says:

> *His kingdom cannot fail, He rules o'er earth and heaven;*
> *The keys of death and hell are to our Jesus given:*
> *Lift up your heart; lift up your voice!*
> *Rejoice, again I say, rejoice!*

Interestingly, this entry appeared in Charles's journal a few years later, on Sunday, July 13, 1746: *At St. Ives no one offered to make the least disturbance. Indeed, the whole place is outwardly changed in this respect. I walk the streets with astonishment, scarce believing it St. Ives. It is the same throughout all the county. All opposition falls before us. . . .*

## VERSE OF THE WEEK

Rejoice greatly, O daughter of Zion!
Shout, O daughter of Jerusalem!
Behold, your King is coming to you.

—Zechariah 9:9

## REFLECT

. . . . . . . . . . . . . . . . . . . . . . . . . . . . . . . . . . . . . . .

Charles Wesley's diary entry dramatically recounts violence that broke out while he was preaching. Recall a time when you were in the midst of chaos. What was your reaction?

_____

_____

_____

_____

How is this hymn's emphasis on God's sovereignty hopeful in times of stress?

_____

_____

_____

_____

What word is repeated in Philippians 4:4 that's also repeated in the chorus of this hymn?

_____

_____

_____

What line does the hymn borrow from Lamentations 3:41?

_____

_____

_____

> _God, the King eternal, who dividest the day from the darkness, and turnest the shadow of death into the morning: drive far off from me all wrong desires, incline my heart to keep Thy law, and guide my feet into the way of peace; that having done Thy will with cheerfulness while it was day, I may, when the night cometh, rejoice to give Thee thanks; through Jesus Christ our Lord. Amen._
> —BOOK OF COMMON PRAYER (1928)[10]

## PRAYER REQUESTS FOR THE WEEK

_____

_____

# Come, Thou Long-Expected Jesus

Charles Wesley

Rowland H. Prichard

1. Come, Thou long expected Jesus,
From our fears and sins release us,
2. Born Thy people to deliver,
Born to reign in us forever,

Born to set Thy people free;
Let us find our rest in Thee.
Born a Child and yet a King;
Now Thy gracious kingdom bring.

Israel's strength and consolation, Hope of all the
By Thine own eternal Spirit, Rule in all our

earth Thou art; Dear desire of every
hearts alone; By Thine all-sufficient

nation, Joy of every longing heart.
merit, Raise us to Thy glorious throne.

# COME, THOU LONG-EXPECTED JESUS

1744

It's hard to imagine the difficulties faced by John and Charles Wesley and their fellow evangelists as they traveled by horseback from town to town, facing mobs and enduring harsh conditions and severe weather. Here is a sampling from Charles's journal as he pressed into Wales in March of 1748:

Wed., March 23rd. I was . . . not to set out till past seven. The continual rain and sharp wind were full in my teeth. I rode all day in great misery, and had a restless, painful night at Tan-y-bwlch.

Thur., March 24th. I resolved to push for Garth, finding my strength would never hold out for three more days riding. At five [a.m.], I set out in hard rain, which continued all day. We went through perils of water. I was quite gone when we came at night to a little village. There was no fire in the poor hut. A brother supplied us with some, nailed up our window, and helped us to bed. I had no more rest than the night before.

Fri., March 25th. I took horse again at five, the rain attending us still. . . . The weather grew more severe. The violent wind drove the hard rain full in our faces. I rode till I could ride no more; walked the last hour; and by five dropped down at Garth.

Charles's primary purpose in going to Garth was to preach, but he had another motive as well. It was to see Miss Sally Gwynne, whom he wanted to marry. Marriage required a regular income, however, and Sally's parents were concerned about Charles's ability to sustain a family with no regular source of finances. Charles agreed to publish two volumes of his *Hymns and Sacred Poems*.

The income from royalties more than satisfied Sally's parents, and the two were married on Saturday, April 8, 1749.

"Come, Thou Long-Expected Jesus" wasn't introduced in this two-volume set of *Hymns and Sacred Songs* containing a total of 455 hymns. It had been published earlier, in a 1745 edition of Christmas hymns entitled *Hymns for the Nativity of Our Lord*. This little hymnal contained eighteen Christmas carols Charles had written, of which "Come, Thou Long-Expected Jesus" is the best known.

## VERSE OF THE WEEK

You therefore must endure hardship as a good soldier of
Jesus Christ.

—2 Timothy 2:3

# REFLECT

What were some of the hardships faced
by Charles Wesley as an evangelist
traveling by horse into Wales?

_____

_____

_____

_____

_____

What does 2 Timothy 2:3 say about
hardships?

_____

_____

_____

_____

_____

This song is best known as a Christmas carol. Does it resonate with you regardless of the time of year? How and why?

_____

_____

_____

How is Jesus the "joy of every longing heart"?

_____

_____

_____

> *Almighty God, give me wisdom to perceive You, intelligence to understand You, diligence to seek You, patience to wait for You, eyes to behold You, a heart to meditate upon You and life to proclaim You, through the power of the Spirit of our Lord Jesus Christ. Amen.*
> —BENEDICT OF NURSIA (C. 480–543)

## PRAYER REQUESTS FOR THE WEEK

_____

_____

# O Come, O Come, Emmanuel

Latin Hymn, 9th cent.
Translated by John M. Neale

Thomas Helmore

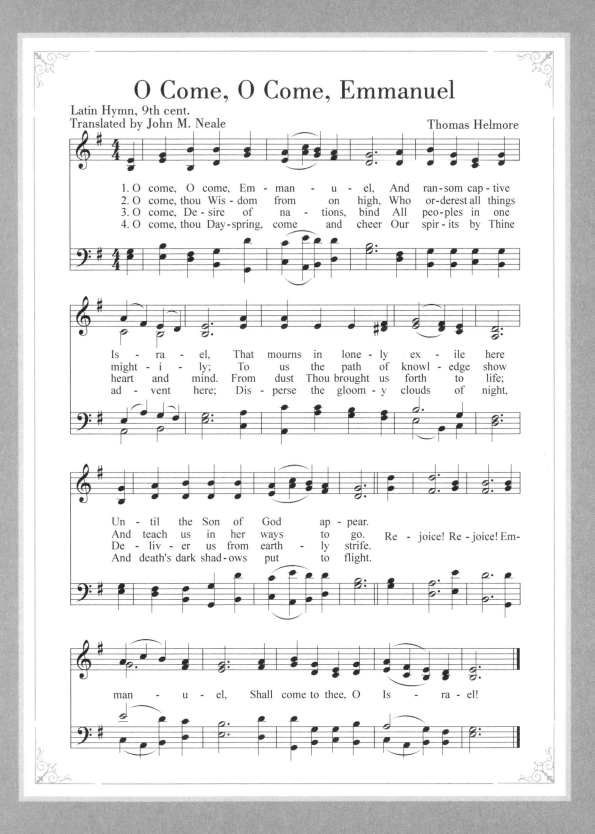

1. O come, O come, Em - man - u - el, And ran-som cap - tive
2. O come, thou Wis - dom from on high, Who or-derest all things
3. O come, De - sire of na - tions, bind All peo-ples in one
4. O come, thou Day-spring, come and cheer Our spir - its by Thine

Is - ra - el, That mourns in lone - ly ex - ile here
might - i - ly; To us the path of knowl - edge show
heart and mind. From dust Thou brought us forth to life;
ad - vent here; Dis - perse the gloom - y clouds of night,

Un - til the Son of God ap - pear.
And teach us in her ways to go.      Re - joice! Re - joice! Em -
De - liv - er us from earth - ly strife.
And death's dark shad - ows put to flight.

man - u - el, Shall come to thee, O Is - ra - el!

# O COME, O COME, EMMANUEL

1851

The origins of this plaintive carol date to medieval times. In the 800s, a series of Latin hymns were sung each day during Christmas Vespers from December 17 to 23. Each of these hymns began with the word "O" and were called the "Great" or "O" Antiphons (the word *antiphon* meaning psalm or anthem). These hymns were apparently restructured into verse form in the 1100s, and finally published in Latin in 1710. In the mid-1800s, they were discovered by an English minister named John Mason Neale, who wove together segments of them to produce the first draft of "O Come, O Come, Emmanuel," which was published in 1851. Neale's original version said, "Draw nigh, draw nigh, Emmanuel."

Neale is a man worth knowing. He was born in London on January 24, 1818, the son of an evangelical Anglican clergyman. He attended Cambridge University and proved to be a brilliant student and prizewinning poet. While there, Neale was influenced by the Oxford Movement and became attracted to Roman Catholicism. In 1841, he was ordained into the Anglican ministry; but his poor health and Catholic leanings prevented him from gaining a parish ministry.

He was appointed instead as the director of Sackville College, a home for old men. (Sackville College, started by Robert Sackville, Earl of Dorset, in the early 1600s as a home for the elderly, is still going strong today in East Grinstead, Sussex.) This was the perfect job for Neale, for he was a compassionate man with a great heart for the needy, but he was also a scholar needing time for research and writing.

As a high church traditionalist, Neale disliked the hymns of Isaac Watts and longed to return Christianity to the liturgical dignity of church history. He was an outspoken advocate of returning church buildings to their former glory. He campaigned, for example, against certain types of stoves that spoiled the tastefulness and charm of English churches. He also worked hard to translate ancient Greek and Latin hymns into English.

In today's hymnals, we find Neale and Watts side by side, the old differences having been forgotten. We owe a debt of gratitude to John Mason Neale every time we sing one of his Christmas carols: "Good King Wenceslas," "O Come, O Come, Emmanuel," "Good Christian Men, Rejoice," and his Palm Sunday hymn, "All Glory, Laud, and Honor."

Behold, the virgin shall be with child, and bear a Son, and they shall call His name Immanuel.

—MATTHEW 1:23

# REFLECT

The author calls this a "plaintive" (meaning sad or mournful) hymn. Does it make you feel sad?

_____

_____

_____

_____

_____

We learn that this hymn is actually a translation with Latin origins from the 800s sung during Christmas Vespers. Does it feel outdated or does it feel holy to you?

_____

_____

_____

_____

"Emmanuel" means "God with us," so this hymn opens with a request for God's presence. How is this a request worth repeating often?

_____

_____

_____

If we only sing this song at Christmastime, how might we be missing out on a blessing?

_____

_____

_____

> *O Wisdom, coming forth from the mouth of the Most High, and reaching mightily from one end of the earth to the other, ordering all things well: come and teach us the way of prudence. . . . O Daystar, splendor of light eternal and sun of righteousness: come and enlighten those who dwell in darkness and the shadow of death. . . . O Emmanuel, our King and Lawgiver, the desire of all nations and their Savior: come and save us, O Lord our God. Amen.*
> —CATHOLIC LITURGY (9TH C.)

## PRAYER REQUESTS FOR THE WEEK

_____

_____

# Praise God, from Whom All Blessings Flow

Thomas Ken

att. to Louis Bourgeois

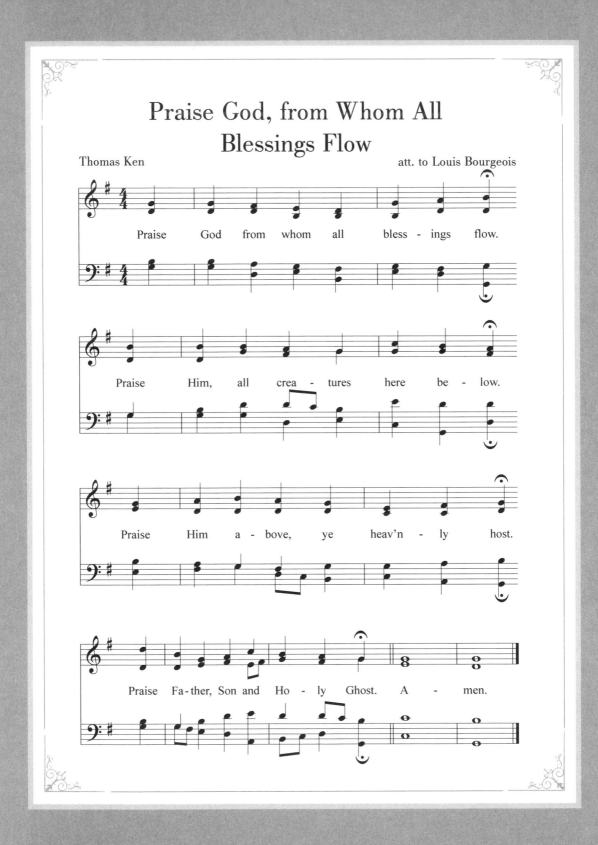

# PRAISE GOD, FROM WHOM ALL BLESSINGS FLOW

### 1674

Before Charles Wesley or Isaac Watts, there was Thomas Ken, who has been called "England's first hymnist." He was born in 1637 in Little Berkhampstead on the fringes of greater London. When his parents died, he was raised by his half sister and her husband who enrolled him in Winchester College, a historic boys' school. Thomas was later ordained to the ministry and returned to Winchester as a chaplain.

To encourage the devotional habits of the boys, Thomas wrote three hymns in 1674. This was revolutionary because English hymns had not yet appeared. Only the psalms were sung in public worship. Ken suggested the boys use the hymns privately in their rooms.

One hymn was to be sung upon waking, another at bedtime, and a third at midnight if sleep didn't come. His morning hymn had thirteen stanzas, beginning with:

*Awake, my soul, and with the sun thy daily stage of duty run;*
*Shake off dull sloth and joyful rise, to pay thy morning sacrifice.*

His evening hymn, equally meaningful, included this verse:

*All praise to Thee, my God, this night, for all the blessings of the light!*
*Keep me, O keep me, King of kings, beneath Thine own almighty wings.*

All three hymns ended with a common stanza, which has since become the most widely sung verse in the world.

*Praise God, from whom all blessings flow; / Praise Him, all creatures here below.*
*Praise Him above, ye heav'nly host; / Praise Father, Son, and Holy Ghost.*

In 1680, Thomas was appointed chaplain to England's King Charles II. It was a thankless job, as Charles kept a variety of mistresses. Once the king asked to lodge a mistress in the chaplain's residence. Thomas rebuked him, saying, "Not for the King's Kingdom!" Afterward the king referred to him as "that little man who refused lodging to poor Nellie."

During the reign of the next king, James II, Thomas, by now a bishop, was sent to the Tower of London for his Protestant convictions. After his release, Thomas retired to the home of a wealthy friend where he died on March 11, 1711. He was buried at sunrise, and the Doxology was sung at his funeral.

Blessed be the God and Father of our Lord Jesus Christ, who has blessed us with every spiritual blessing in the heavenly places in Christ.

—EPHESIANS 1:3

# REFLECT

. . . . . . . . . . . . . . . . . . . . . . . . . . . . . . . . . . . .

Why is author Thomas Ken called "England's first hymnist"?

_____

_____

_____

_____

_____

What was so revolutionary about Thomas Ken teaching the boys at Winchester the three hymns he'd written?

_____

_____

_____

_____

_____

How did Thomas Ken suffer for his convictions? If you're so led, lift up a prayer for someone suffering today for their faith.

_____

_____

_____

Read Psalm 16. What does it reveal about receiving blessings in our relationship with God?

_____

_____

_____

> *O Lord, move my heart with the calm, smooth flow of Your grace. Let the river of Your love run through my soul. May my soul be carried by the current of Your love, towards the wide, infinite ocean of heaven. Stretch out my heart with Your strength, as You stretch out the sky above the earth. Smooth out any wrinkles of hatred or resentment. Enlarge my soul that it may know more fully Your truth. Amen.*
>
> —GILBERT OF HOYLAND (D. 1170)

## PRAYER REQUESTS FOR THE WEEK

_____

_____

# NOTES

1. Information for this segment came from John Stoughton, *Philip Doddridge: His Life and Labors* (London: Jackson and Walford, 1852).
2. Taken from Robert J. Morgan, *On This Day* (Nashville: Thomas Nelson Publishers, 1997), installment for November 4.
3. See the story behind the hymn "Search Me, O God" on page 151.
4. Selections from the *Book of Common Prayer* are treated as public domain by the Episcopal Church.
5. The beautiful building of Edinburgh's Free High Church was vacated by its members in 1934, and now serves as the library for the University of Edinburgh. It is obvious to anyone who enters the library that it was originally a church.
6. Sankey wrote the original version of his combined autobiography and hymn history in Battle Creek, Michigan, where he was recovering from illness. Unfortunately, a fire broke out and destroyed his one and only manuscript, along with all his collected notes. Greatly depressed, Sankey, who was blind by then, dictated *My Life and the Story of the Gospel Hymns* from memory, relying on scraps of information, as best he could. It is still an amazing book.
7. More than one hundred of these notebooks are now in the George C. Stebbins Memorial Collection, housed in the Rare Book Library of Washington's National Cathedral.
8. Taken from Morgan, *On This Day*, installment for May 7.
9. Marvin L. Lubenow, *Bones of Contention* (Grand Rapids: Baker Book House, 1992), 77. I am indebted to Lubenow for much of the information in this story, gleaned from chapter 6 of this excellent book, subtitled *A Creationist Assessment of Human Fossils*.
10. *Book of Common Prayer*, public domain.

# INDEX—ALPHABETICAL BY TITLE

# INDEX—AUTHOR/SONGWRITER

# INDEX—FIRST LINE OF HYMN

# ABOUT THE AUTHOR

Robert J. Morgan is a writer and speaker who serves as the teaching pastor at The Donelson Fellowship in Nashville. He is the author of *The Red Sea Rules*; *Worry Less, Live More*; *The Strength You Need*; *100 Bible Verses That Made America*; the Then Sings My Soul series; and many other titles, with more than 4.5 million copies in circulation. He is available to speak at conferences and conventions. He and his late wife, Katrina, have three daughters and sixteen grandchildren.

Robertjmorgan.com